Congress United States

Proceedings on the Death of Hon. Solomon Foot

Including the Addresses delivered in the Senate and House of

Representatives on April 12, 1866

Congress United States

Proceedings on the Death of Hon. Solomon Foot
Including the Addresses delivered in the Senate and House of Representatives on
April 12, 1866

ISBN/EAN: 9783337175054

Printed in Europe, USA, Canada, Australia, Japan

Cover: Foto ©Suzi / pixelio.de

More available books at **www.hansebooks.com**

PROCEEDINGS

ON THE

DEATH OF HON. SOLOMON FOOT,

INCLUDING THE

ADDRESSES

DELIVERED IN THE

SENATE AND HOUSE OF REPRESENTATIVES

ON

THURSDAY, APRIL 12, 1866.

WASHINGTON:
GOVERNMENT PRINTING OFFICE.
1866.

PROCEEDINGS

ON THE

DEATH OF HON. SOLOMON FOOT.

IN THE SENATE OF THE UNITED STATES,
WEDNESDAY, MARCH 28, 1866.

Remarks of Mr. SUMNER, of Massachusetts.

Mr. PRESIDENT: A great bereavement has fallen upon the Senate. Mr. FOOT, a senator of Vermont, one of our most honored associates, and the oldest among us in continuous service, died this morning at 8 o'clock. He has passed from this scene of duty and of honor. In the presence of such a sorrow it seems better that public business should be suspended in this chamber for to-day. Accordingly, I shall make a motion which I believe will have the sympathetic concurrence of the Senate. I make it in the absence of the surviving senator of Vermont, who is now necessarily engaged in attendance upon the family of the deceased, and after consultation with him. I move that the Senate do now adjourn.

The motion was unanimously agreed to, and the Senate adjourned.

THURSDAY, MARCH 29, 1866.
Remarks of Mr. POLAND, of Vermont.

Mr. PRESIDENT: I rise to perform a most painful duty. A very few months since Vermont was represented in the Senate of the United States by two of her most distinguished citizens, of large ability, tried integrity, and filled with the wisdom derived from long experience in public affairs. Just previous to the commencement of the present session one of these eminent men, my predecessor on this floor, was called away by death. While the voices of mourning for his loss are yet sounding in our ears, the bolt has again fallen, and Vermont is again called to weep over the dead form of the other. My colleague in this body, and one of its oldest and most distinguished members, the Hon. SOLOMON FOOT, died at his lodgings in this city yesterday, at about eight o'clock in the morning. He endured a long and painful sickness with patience and resignation, and departed this life with bright and cheerful hopes of a blessed immortality in the life to come. The time which has elapsed since this great sorrow has fallen upon us has been so short, that amid the grief and care occasioned by the sad event, I have found no time in which to prepare to speak suitably of the character and distinguished public services of our departed associate; and I shall therefore ask the indulgence of the Senate on some future day, when time shall have a little dulled the sharp edge of our grief, for myself and others who may desire an opportunity to pay appropriate tribute to the memory of the deceased.

I now offer the following resolutions, and ask their present consideration :

Resolved, That the members of the Senate, from a sincere desire of showing every mark of respect to the Hon. Solomon Foot, deceased, late a senator from the State of Vermont, will go into mourning for the residue of the present session by the usual mode of wearing crape on the left arm.

Resolved, That the Senate will attend the funeral of the deceased from the Senate chamber at 1 o'clock to-day; and that the committee of arrangements, consisting of Messrs. Doolittle, Anthony, Howard, Hendricks, Sherman, and Buckalew, superintend the same.

Ordered, That the Secretary communicate these proceedings to the House of Representatives.

The resolutions were unanimously adopted.

THE FUNERAL CEREMONIES.

Sermon by Rev. BYRON SUNDERLAND, D. D.

At 1 o'clock p. m., on the 29th of March, the corps, attended by the committee of arrangements, pall-bearers, family and friends of the deceased, and citizens of Vermont, was removed from the late residence of the deceased, and placed in the area in the centre of the Senate chamber, where seats were provided for the remaining senator and representatives from Vermont, and the family of the deceased. The judges and officers of the Supreme Court of the United States, the President of the United States, and the heads of the various departments, and the members of the House of Representatives, preceded by their Speaker and officers, entered the Senate chamber at intervals, and were conducted to the seats assigned to them.

The pall-bearers were senators Fessenden, Harris, Johnson, Guthrie, Lane of Indiana, and Sumner Lieutenant General Grant and other officers of the army commingled in the solemn scene. The Rev. E. H. Gray, D. D., Chaplain of the Senate, and the Rev. C. B. Boynton, Chaplain of the House of Representatives, officiated in the devotional services; and the Rev. Byron Sunderland, D. D., delivered the following discourse over the bier :

"Like as a father pitieth his children, so the Lord pitieth them that fear him. For he knoweth our frame; he remembereth that we are dust. As for man, his days are as grass; as a flower of the field, so he flourisheth, for the wind passeth over it and it is gone, and the place thereof shall know it no more. But the mercy of the Lord is from everlasting to everlasting upon them that fear him; and his righteousness unto children's children, to such as keep his covenant, and to those that remember his commandments to do them."—*Psalm* ciii, 13–18.

There is no need, on this solemn occasion, to make an exposition of this language or to build an argument upon it. Interpreted by the dispensation of Providence which convenes us here to-day in this high place of the nation, at this anxious period of our public affairs, it becomes a sermon in itself, plainly speaking home to every heart its great lessons of instruction, of admonition, and of consolation. Here is the fatherhood of God and the frailty of man. Here is omnipotence directed by compassion to shield and save the creatures that must otherwise perish without a remedy and without a hope; here is divine, illimitable fidelity encouraging and assuring human weakness and waywardness to seek in the paths of virtue and of piety that secure possession which may outlast all the fleeting trifles of time, and remain forever in the presence and favor of Jehovah, when the earth shall have crumbled, and the firmament shall have been rolled together as a scroll.

Would that now we, in this funeral hour, might lay aside the conventional and proper pomps of this Senate chamber, as we have been willing to arrest the momentous tide of the daily affairs that are pressing upon us here, in order to pay our respect to the memory of one so long an honored member of the Senate of the United States, but whom God has now removed from these scenes of earth; would that here and now, with his sacred ashes in our midst, and all the signals of our bereavement displayed before us, we might forget the tasks and the anxieties, the strifes and conflicts, the exciting questions and startling changes of this great time, and go back again to the feelings and the days of our early childhood. Oh! could we become this day for a little space as once we were— the unsophisticated and comparatively unsoiled children of those purer years, while habits were unformed and associations were unfixed, and when our minds could perceive and our hearts could feel more keenly than now they may the great truths of home and parentage, of the soul and religion, of God and immortality, of Jesus and the resurrection. And why should we not be so, for youth has its wisdom as well as mature age, and the simplicity of childhood is often clearer than the worldly discretion of many years.

Senators, Representatives, Friends : I do not come to make a great plea this day before you. I do not come to analyze or eulogize that noble life which has just been concluded in your midst. I have no

thought of reviewing the public history of those events in which he
has borne with yourselves so conspicuous a part. But I come rather
as an humble son of that State in this great Union which gave us a
like birth beneath its mountains, and inspired us with its pure and po-
tent airs of liberty : I come rather because, in the providence of God,
it has been allotted to me, as his pastor and friend in Washington, to
be near and to know him well for many years: I come because invited,
generously invited, by my brother in the ministry of reconciliation,
also of our native State, and Chaplain of the Senate of the United
States, and because it has been told me that I should thus fulfil a
desire of family and friends, both here and elsewhere, to speak for
him who once and so short a time ago could speak for others here
with most impressive eloquence, but whose lips, alas! too mute, are
silent on earth forever.

I only come to tell the simple story of his going out from among
us. It may be possible that the details I have to give will seem to
some too delicate, too sacred to be rehearsed in public. But I have
long felt that there existed an affectation among many of our public
men, and a factitious modesty, which more conceals the truth of God
than fosters any genuine good taste. And now, under the sanction
of the sacred passage I have read to you, and as another solemn and
impressive instance of its reality and truthfulness, I propose to follow the developments of the experience of our departed friend from
the commencement to the close of his last illness and the conclusion
of his mortal career.

Senator Foot, as chairman of the Senate committee to make
arrangements for observing the anniversary of the birthday of President Lincoln, on the 12th of February, 1866, in the hall of the
House of Representatives, was actively engaged on that day in the
performance of the duties assigned to him. The following night he
suffered severely from an attack of internal inflammation, which was,
however, arrested by the prompt attention of his physician, and he
had in a day or two so far recovered as to visit the Senate chamber
once more, where his last official work appears to have been the
offering of the appropriate resolutions which closed the action of the

Senate in reference to the solemn and imposing ceremonies of the 12th of February. But meanwhile another more permanent difficulty appeared, and jaundice, with general prostration of the physical powers and mental dejection, was the consequence. It was not supposed by his physicians or friends that his case was at all dangerous or alarming, while, of course, anxiety was felt to see him fully recovered and able to resume his duties. But from the first he himself seems to have been impressed with the conviction that it would be his last sickness, and this conviction he freely and at all times expressed. It is not the design of these brief fragments to give a complete history of the case as it went on from day to day to its final termination. I have a desire simply to record some of the incidents of the last illness of Senator Foot, which may serve to show the state of his mind on the subject of religious faith and experience, and also his ideas and prospects of a future state. I only profess to give the substance of interviews at which I was present. This outline will be necessarily fragmentary; but so far as it goes I believe it to state truly, and often exactly in the language employed, the incidents here narrated.

Having called upon him two or three times before he was confined to his bed, I saw him only in company with many other friends, who were going and coming at will, and the conversation at these times was general, with no special reference to the subject of religion.

But on Saturday evening, March 10, on calling at his rooms, at Mrs. Carter's, on Capitol Hill, I found he was then in bed, and that the disease had proved more difficult of treatment than was at first supposed. He had suffered at times intensely. After speaking with him for a few moments about the symptoms of his case, and the prospect of fully meeting them by the remedies employed, I rose to take my leave of him, saying, "My dear Senator, it is little I can do to help you or testify my gratitude and affection for you; but there is one thing I can do and shall continue to do, and that is to pray for you." He immediately replied, "Yes, that is what I want you to do—what I want you to do *now;*" then asking his wife, who stood at the foot of the bed, to close the door and come and join us in our supplication, we for the first time so knelt together in that chamber of sickness and poured out our desires to God. He seemed very grateful to have such a season of worship, and bade me "good-by" for the night. The next time I called, and indeed for two or three times after, he was so engaged with others arranging his affairs, or trying to obtain rest, that I did not speak with him. But on Monday, March 19, I had an interview with him at his own request. When we were alone, with the door shut, he always insisted on the door being shut whenever religious subjects were to be considered, perhaps in deference to the command of Christ, "When thou hast entered into thy closet, shut to thy door,") he commenced by saying that he had desired to see and converse with me; that he had received a very tender and affecting letter from his old friend and pastor, the Rev. Dr. Aiken, of Rutland, Vermont, on the subject of his spiritual welfare; and, continuing to speak with great solemnity and earnestness, frequently interrupted by weeping and sobbing, he said : "I know it is but a poor time for a man to pay attention to the concerns of his soul when he is brought face to face with death. And I can say, that having always assented, intellectually, at least, to the truth of the Christian doctrines, I have only been too prone to postpone the practical question for so long a time to find at last, what I now have to lament, that life has been wasted in not having been devoted to life's greatest end. This thought, indeed, has more deeply impressed me for the last two years; and at the commencement of this illness I was about proposing to assume a duty long neglected, but which I have felt that I would take up in hope of receiving some further light and strength from the only source of our help—that is, from our Maker and God. The duty I refer to is that of family worship morning and evening, day by day. For years I have daily read the Bible in the presence of my wife; but when I have seen her seeking her God in prayer so habitually and earnestly, I have felt that we ought to be united in it, and have purposed, if ever permitted to do so, that this privilege as well as duty shall no longer be neglected."

Continuing, he said, "I feel that I can never be thankful enough to God for giving me a pious ancestry. My father and mother were both devoted Christians, and I was fully instructed in early childhood in the lessons of the Gospel of Jesus Christ. I have never doubted from that day to this the truth and reality of those teachings. I know and feel that I am a sinner. I believe that Christ made an atonement sufficient for all men, and that this atonement is the only ground of salvation for human beings. I am well convinced that none will ever be saved by the works of righteousness which they have done. I have a strong desire to accept these terms of mercy, if only I might have an assurance that God will not now reject me after my long rejection of Him. That is the point to which I have come. Is there anything for me to do that I have not done, and will you point out the way, that I may go onward in it?" In commencing a reply to this appeal, I adverted to the fact that I had long had a desire for such an interview as this, and expressed a thankful sense that it had been so graciously accorded at this time, and I was going on to state, by way of evidencing still further the tokens of Divine favor granted to himself and his friends in the long, upright, useful life he had been enabled to lead, and, judging by the standard of men, in the comparatively pure and noble example he had given both in private and public relations to his fellow-countrymen, and especially the young men of this generation in our land, that this was now and ever would be a source of satisfaction to his family and friends, and to the people of his town and State—when misapprehending the object of my remarks, and supposing I was about to lead him to rely upon his past life and character for his future prospects, he quickly interposed to say, "All that will not answer me now. I must have a heart-work. I must have the foundation of the atonement of Christ alone to stand upon. I know there is no other name given under heaven or among men whereby we must be saved." Then leaving the topic on which I was speaking, I tried to address myself to the one point which I discovered to be weighing upon his mind, and that was how he should be saved simply and solely upon the plan of God's grace through faith in the Lord Jesus. I explained to him, by reference to my own experience, the nature of saving faith, and the difficulties I found in exercising it. I instructed him in the distinctions that exist between the full submission and surrender of the soul to God and those expectations which often attend this surrender—expectations of some vivid token or manifestation from God that we are accepted of Him, and expectations which are generally doomed to disappointment, simply because they originate in a misapprehension of the gracious work of God's spirit in the soul, and are in nowise necessary to the progress or perfection of that work, the first thing of all being the very surrender itself, which cuts off all expectation; and all the work which man can do is summed up in those two familiar lines, so often sung by Christians:

Here, Lord, I give myself away
'Tis all that I can do.

I then endeavored to turn his mind away from the thought of expecting to the simple work of submitting and surrendering all into the hands of God, and distinctly made the proposal that he should now, in the spirit of a little child and with unquestioning confidence, commit all the interests of his entire being, for time and eternity, to God, and asked if he would join me in a prayer thus consecrating him forever to the Lord; to which he earnestly and promptly assented. After prayer I gave him some further counsel, designed to aid him in keeping to the solemn dedication of his soul to God which had just been made, and after an interview somewhat protracted I took my leave of him for the time.

I then visited him daily for several days, watching the development of what I cannot doubt was the gracious work of God's Holy Spirit begun and progressing in the soul; and in those subsequent interviews I perceived that he was becoming more and more like a little child, his faith more simple, and consequently more strong. He said at length "that he thought he had found the way." "I have," he continued, "been thinking much of those two lines repeated the other day:

'Here, Lord, I give myself away;
''Tis all that I can do.'

I begin to understand that this comprehends all, and I am beginning
to lean alone on Jesus Christ as my Saviour and friend." I repeated
to him several of the promises of the Bible, on which his mind seemed
to fasten with evident satisfaction. On one occasion he commenced
by saying, as I approached his bedside, " Well, my dear minister,
here I still am, trying to do two things—trying to get well and trying to prepare to die." I told him " that though the issue was in
God's hands, yet I had strong hopes this sickness would not be unto
death ; that it seemed to me to be rather but another mercy of the
Lord in disguise, to give him that time for meditation and prayer
which it would be impossible otherwise in the circumstances of his
position to obtain, and that when the moral purposes of his Heavenly
Father had been accomplished he would then be restored to his customary walks in life, with an experience of affliction sanctified to his
highest good." But to this he made in substance his unvarying
reply, " That he could not divest himself of the conviction that he
would not recover." It seemed useless to try to shake his conclusion in this respect, and I left him on that day resolved not to renew
the attempt.

On Thursday, the 22d of March, there was an evident progress in
his spiritual experience, and I began now to think that his feet were
surely planted upon the Rock, and his hope was being confirmed.
On alluding to the effect of faith in Christ upon the mind, and
quoting to him the words from the 5th of Romans, " Therefore being
justified by faith, we have peace with God through our Lord Jesus
Christ," he spoke out in answer, as if carrying forward the conclusion of the apostle, by repeating the following most suitable and
affecting lines :

> " Jesus, the vision of thy face
> Hath overpowering charms ;
> I shall not fear death's cold embrace
> If Christ be in my arms.
> Then while ye hear my heartstrings break,
> How sweet my minutes roll,
> A mortal paleness on my cheek,
> And glory in my soul."

Then, after prayer, in which he renewedly dedicated himself to God, I again took leave of him. After this my interviews for the remainder of that week were shorter, with less of incident than those that had preceded, but of the same general character. During this time I had been in conference with the Chaplain of the Senate, the Rev. Dr. Gray, who had called several times, in the interest and anxiety he felt for the spiritual welfare of our friend, and for whom Senator Foot entertained the warmest regard.

Thus he continued until Monday, March 26, when the symptoms of his case became more alarming. The day before (being Sunday) he had informed his friends it would be the last Sunday he should spend with them on earth. Nothing then appeared to indicate a change for the worse, and his friends received the suggestion as but another proof of the mental depression so natural to disease of this specific type. On this day, therefore, the physicians became alarmed, and at one time it was thought he might not survive even a few hours. But, rallying again, the feeble powers of nature made a stand, and in the evening he seemed somewhat revived. I did not see him during the day. But on Tuesday morning, March 27, I repaired early to his chamber, arriving about 9 o'clock, and, with a short time of absence, remaining until about the hour of 6 o'clock in the evening. This was the last day with him on earth. As if forewarned of his approaching end, he spent the whole day in receiving and parting with his friends, and performing his last acts of religious devotion. For several hours he talked almost incessantly, until he seemed to have finished his work and was ready to depart. As I approached him in the morning there were none present at the moment but members of the family, and I proposed we should have a season of prayer. "Oh, yes," he immediately exclaimed, "that is what I want—close the door—shut it tight—and come then and kneel down and pray here. All kneel down; all pray—pray that my faith may be strengthened; that my heart may be renewed; that my sins may be forgiven through that one atonement of Jesus Christ; that my views of it may be clear; that I may see in it a sufficiency for the sins of the whole world, and particularly for my sins, which have been so many and

so aggravated during a long life, that they may all be cleansed away
and remembered no more!"

Then after prayer he repeated again, at our request, the lines
already quoted, and with great emphasis and appreciation. It was
now 10 o'clock, and the tidings that he was sinking brought many
of his friends to his bedside, among whom was the Secretary of State,
the Secretary of War, several of the senators and others of the Senate, the members of the Vermont delegation and others of the House
of Representatives, and many other persons in private life. About
12 o'clock Dr. Baxter, one of his physicians, came in and took him
by the hand with an emotion which he could not conceal from the
quick notice of the dying statesman. As if clearly reading the
thoughts of his friend, while sorrow was so deeply depicted on his
countenance, he immediately began to address him in language of the
most touching confidence and gratitude, and recalled many an affecting reminiscence of his past intercourse with the members of his
family, especially with his father and himself. On my again approaching him he commenced by recalling the year and place
of my birth, and saying that at that time and in that place he
was a youth in his academic studies preparing for a college
course. When the friend at whose house he had been for
years during his stay in Washington came into his chamber
he immediately called her by name, recounted her care for him,
and loaded her with the most affecting assurances of thankful-
ness.

A few moments after, at the request of a friend, and when the
numbers present had somewhat diminished, he repeated for the third
time, and with his hands so placed together as if to emphasize and
impress them, the striking and impressive verses already quoted, and
then said, "Sing them; I like to hear the voice of sacred singing; it
bears me up as on the air of heaven." And to a suggestion that he
might be wearied by so many visits, so much excitement and talking,
he said, "No, it does not hurt me; I rather desire it; I am borne up
as on angels' wings; it is no effort for me to converse or hear you
speaking." On the renewal of his wish to hear the singing we were

obliged to change the words he had repeated for that beautiful and now familiar hymn—

"Just as I am—without one plea."

As we sang this he lay as if entranced by it, and suddenly perceiving all present in tears, and his wife sobbing, her head bowed upon his hand in the grief of her affection, he said, looking around on the circle, " Why these tears? There is no occasion for weeping. This is heaven begun below ! I am only going home a little sooner, that is all." At the conclusion of the hymn, as if repeating the sentiment of the last stanza, he said, " I *do* trust in my Saviour."

A few moments after, when his brother, Dr. Foot, but two years younger than himself, who had arrived a few days before from his home in Canada, and to whom at their first meeting he had expressed the same feeling that he should not recover, now came toward him, but, filled with emotion, immediately turned away to conceal it, he said to me in an under tone, " If God has given it to me to leave such a name as my family will not be ashamed to remember, it is not a cause of pride or boasting, but of gratitude to Him only who doeth all things well; and if when I am gone they shall sometimes think of me, and mention me as belonging to them, it will prove that I have at least studied not to give them pain."

To Mrs. Browning, a trusted friend in the house, he said : " I am glad to see you this morning ; these earthly partings are severe, but there are no tears, no sorrows in heaven. There we shall meet, I trust, ere long."

To Mrs. Woodbridge, Mr. DeWitt Clarke, the Hon. Messrs. Morrill and Baxter, and several others in humbler life, from Vermont, who came during the day to inquire after his condition, and receive his dying testimony, he addressed the most tender and affecting words.

To his colleague, Senator Poland, who had just assumed in the Senate the seat of the lamented Collamer, and who, boarding in the same house, and having a room almost adjacent to his chamber, was several times by his bedside during the day, with a concern speaking in his face for the anticipated loss of his dying friend which none could fail to read, he committed in a special manner the great trusts of their position in the Senate, saying: "I have finished my work as a representative from Vermont in the councils of the nation, and now, my dear colleague, it will be for you and my successor in office faithfully to represent the people of our State and worthily to discharge the high responsibility they have thus imposed upon you. I doubt not you will do this to the satisfaction of the people not only in our State, but throughout the country."

When Senator Doolittle approached his bedside, he immediately stretched out his hand and said: "Dear brother, you have always been kind to me—a dear, good brother senator; I can never reward you, but you know where your reward lies. You have long been a professor of the religion of the Gospel. You know what it is to enjoy its consolations in sickness and in health. The mercy of God has been very great to me in this sickness. I have so many kind friends, so many angelic ministers all around me. It seems as though a company of angels were all about me, and hovering over me, to bear up a sinking spirit from its mortality." Then, after a pause, as if reviewing his past life and endeavoring to recall its conflicts, he said, "I have been trying to call to mind if there was a human being on earth to whom I have intentionally done wrong or injustice. If there is, I pray God to forgive me." And on another occasion during the day he said, "If I have an enemy in the world, I thank God I do not know it."

When Secretary Stanton entered the room, some time about midday, he seemed very much gratified, and said: "You are kind to visit me, Mr. Stanton. I am here yet, living and dying. I have no acute pain, no severe distress; but a general sinking of the system, the constitution breaking up. But I am surrounded by so many kind friends, they seem to bear me up as on angels' wings." The Secretary of War then said to him, "The President had intended to come with me to see you, but has been prevented by pressure of business. If it is possible, however, to visit you to-day, he will do so; but he has delegated me to express to you his kind regards

and sympathies." Not hearing the words distinctly, some one
repeated them, to which he replied : "Oh, yes; if he comes I would
be pleased to see him. It is twenty-three years ago since we first
met. If the President comes I shall be glad to see him. The Secretary always anticipates everything; he is one of the best men I ever
knew ; this world cannot reward him, but there is a God in heaven
who can do so, and I am sure he will not lose that reward. There
is a God on high who will not fail to reward him." Presently he
added, " I have a good deal of physical strength left yet, so that I
might continue perhaps a week, but on that point I do not specu-
late." On the Secretary remarking that "We are all in God's
hands," he responded : "Oh, yes ; and He is dealing with me in
great mercy. The Lord reigns; let the earth rejoice! And well
may God reign, and well may the earth rejoice that he does reign.
That there is a God who reigns over all, there can be no manner of
doubt. We do not come into this world by chance; we are not
creatures of accident. We have been born under a superintending
Providence, and are candidates for a certain immortality." Then
pausing again, as if contemplating his approaching departure, he
said : "When I leave this place, I wish no parade, no ostentatious
demonstrations to be made; only the ordinary proceedings which
custom and propriety impose ; and thus I desire to be borne to my
friends and home in Rutland, Vermont, and laid among the people
who have been so faithful to me—more faithful, I fear, than I have
ever been to them. Let me be sent home to the people who have
done so much for me; they will prepare everything, and there by
them let me be buried." Some one remarked : "And there is your
minister, too." " Yes," he replied, with great warmth of feeling,
"they are both there; the one a venerable man of God, to whom I
have long listened."

Presently Mr. Bassett, the doorkeeper of the Senate, came
in, and was greeted in the same ardent and earnest manner by
the dying senator. He recalled his first meeting with him
fifteen years ago, and testified to his uniform kindness, and said,
" I cannot reward him, but God will do it; and that will be

a far better, higher, more glorious reward than man can ever bestow."

Some one again inquiring if he did not feel great exhaustion and bodily distress, he replied, "Not much distress; this I consider one of my comfortable days." Then turning he saw Mrs. Foot weeping at the foot of the bed, with Mrs. Browning at her side. This seemed to pain him most deeply, and he said, pointing to his wife, "There is my great grief, my beloved wife—to part from her is like tearing the silver cord asunder." On being approached by these ladies, Mrs. Browning remarked "that they had been permitted to enjoy each other's society long on earth, and they indulged the hope that this society would be resumed again in heaven."

"Oh, yes," he answered, "we have been a family long held together, and memory is full of tender visions of the past. God grant they may be renewed in another and better world!"

At this time Senator Fessenden approached him, to whom he eagerly stretched out his hand and said, "My dear friend Fessenden, the man by whose side I have sat so long, whom I have regarded as the model of a statesman and parliamentary leader, on whom I have leaned, and to whom I have looked more than to any other living man for guidance and direction in public affairs, the grief I feel is that the strong tie which has so long bound us together must now be severed. But, my dear Fessenden, if there is memory after death, that memory will be active, and I shall call to mind the whole of our intercourse on earth." The senator thus addressed, too much affected to reply in words, stooped over and kissed the brow of his dying friend, and turned away in silence. Toward evening, when it was intimated that the same senator had returned to inquire after him, and he was asked if he desired to see him, his reply was prompt—"Always," "always." With hands clasped they remained for some time, the enfeebled senator repeating his grateful sense of the friendship so long existing between them, and being in turn assured of its reciprocal estimation by his friend. Some one observing that though parted for a time while on earth, they might have hope of a reunion in the spirit world hereafter: "Oh, yes," he ex-

claimed, with great emphasis, "I believe in God and the life eternal."
And finally, in a tone of affecting tenderness, he bade his friend
"farewell," saying "Good-by, and may God bless you forever-
more."

Afterwards Senator Grimes approached him, to whom he said,
"Ah, my dear friend Grimes, have you come to see me? I have
been through a terrible ordeal here the last six weeks." Then
noticing that all were deeply affected, he added, "Do not cease to
talk; these things cannot alarm me." Then taking the senator by
the hand, he said, "Yes, I know the man, a man about whom there
is no deceit; with whom neither in private nor in public was there a
deceitful thought or a deceitful word." His friend then remarked
that he must have suffered very severely; he replied, "I have supposed that the frailty of human nature could not endure it so long;
and then recurring evidently to scenes of the past in which he had
mingled with his friend, and as if soliloquizing, he added, "He was
one of the first and last and best of my associates, and there was no
mistake about him." Then turning to the senator, he said, as the
latter was about to leave him, "You are not going out of the city?"
On being answered in the negative, they exchanged "farewells,"
and were parted forever upon earth.

To another senator, Mr. Brown, who came in soon after, he said,
"I am glad to see you, my dear associate; you know what it is to
be a disciple of Christ. I hope we shall meet in heaven. This
world is a poor place for saint or sinner to dwell in forever. Its
scenes are passing away; its fashion perishes. There is nothing
steadfast, nothing stable here." And thus he continued for some
time, speaking to one and another, sending last tokens of love to
absent kindred and friends, and doing his last work on earth.

At about half past two o'clock, all being prepared, by his desire
and with the consent of his physician, who was indefatigable in at-
tending to every wish, in the presence of his family and a few Christian friends, he signified his public profession of faith in Christ by
receiving the symbols of the Lord's Supper, and joining, for the
first and last time on earth, in that communion which all God's

children hope to renew in heaven. On receiving the bread into his mouth, he uttered in a slow but solemn and reverential manner these words: "This bread is the symbol of the broken body of Christ Jesus, through whom alone I hope for the mercy of God and the gift of eternal life." This most affecting and solemn scene, only to be appreciated and understood by those who have known experimentally the life which it outwardly sets forth, was concluded by singing the following lines, during which his soul seemed borne away, indeed, as on angels' wings:

> "How firm a foundation, ye saints of the Lord,
> Is laid for your faith in His excellent word!
> What more could he say than to you he hath said,
> You who unto Jesus for refuge have fled—
> The soul that on Jesus hath leaned for repose,
> I will not, I cannot, desert to his foes;
> That soul, though all hell should endeavor to shake,
> I'll never, no, never! no, never forsake!"

After this he seemed to be satisfied, and only awaited the appointed hour of departure.

To Mr. Seward, Secretary of State, who visited him in the after part of the day, he addressed similar words of tenderness, and exchanged with him the affectionate regards of their former friendliness.

Between four and five o'clock a striking scene occurred. Senator Foster, now the President pro tempore of the Senate, and in that office one of Senator Foot's successors, came in to see him. Their interview was peculiarly affecting. The dying man, stretching out his hand to Mr. Foster, drew him to his side, and then addressed him substantially as follows: "My dear friend, we have been sitting in the Senate for years together. I have had for you the warmest regard—confidence in your judgment, respect for your talents, and a personal attachment on which no shadow of unkindness has ever rested. I have always considered you as a pattern of a Christian statesman and a Christian gentleman." On being assured that his sentiments were fully reciprocated, and that all his associates enter-

tained toward him a similar feeling, he answered, that for whatever
of kindness they had felt for him he was sincerely grateful; but,
said he, " I am aware of my imperfections. I may have given them
offence—at times I must have done so. I know I have been a sinner, and it is only of late that I have been able to hope in the par-
doning mercy of God, and to feel my title made sure to that future
inheritance which you, my dear friend, have been so long antici-
pating." After some further similar convesration, Senator Foster,
supposing he might be wearied, was about to take leave of him, and
then, while still their hands were clasped together, as if thinking of
the sainted dead who had gone before, and looking for the last time
into the face of a man who seemed destined so soon to join them, he
said : " I must bid you farewell, in hope that we may meet again in
heaven ;" and stooping down he, too, left a silent, parting kiss on
the brow of his dying friend. As he turned away, with melting
heart and tearful eye, the last words which fell upon his ear from
that couch of mortal weakness were, "Oh, yes; we shall meet
again in heaven, and the time will not be long. Farewell, dear
friend. God bless you evermore !" The impressions borne away
from that chamber of death, and so strikingly expressed by Senator
Foster to the afflicted family as he took his departure, were indeed
such as to rob death of all his terrors, and to cause the living to
have been willing to exchange places if they might also change
prospects with the dying statesman.

But his hours were rapidly running out, and he seemed only too
eager for their conclusion. The day set ; the night wore on. The
morning came again, and all this while he lay peacefully, attended
by gentle women, his kindred, whom he described repeatedly as
ministering angels sent to soothe and comfort him, and make light
his pathway to the tomb. At about seven o'clock on the morning
of Wednesday, the 28th of March, it was evident he could not much
longer survive. Then, as if admonished by some invisible attendant
that his moments were few, he signified his desire to see once more
the light of the sun in heaven, and the Capitol, on which it shone,
and where he had so long served the people of his State and country,

and where his associates would soon again assemble. They lifted him up, but his eyes were already dim. He sank back upon his pillow. Seeing his time was at hand, the words of the 23d Psalm were then read, and a solemn prayer went up from the lips of one, the dearest to him on earth. He called her to his side, and folded her in his arms for a moment; then, as his breathing became choked, he said, "What, can this be death? Is it come already?" Then, lying a few moments longer, with eyes all full of celestial radiance, he lifted his hands and looked up, exclaiming: "I see it! I see it! The gates are wide open! beautiful! beautiful!" and without a movement or pang immediately expired.

I have no apology to offer for dwelling so long on the closing scenes of one whom I loved as a father, and to whom for years past I have learned to look for a father's counsels in many of my earthly affairs. Alas, how many will miss him in all the ranks and conditions of society! How will he be lamented by a bereaved and sorrowing people! They shall tell to whom it more appropriately belongs. Others there are who will make the record of his history, and depict the attributes of his private character, and trace the direction of his public life; others there are who will show his position in the mighty passage of the nation through one of its most eventful and momentous periods; who will gather the garlands for his brow, and erect a monument to his memory. It is ours to derive from the solemn dispensation of Providence, which has thus removed him from our midst, the practical lessons it is so pre-eminently designed to enforce upon us.

1. First we see the difference between Pagan and Christian light. The sentiments of the ancients and of heathen sages now are and were exceedingly uncertain, clouded, and obscure in respect to a future state, and the conditions of happiness therein. Their hopes, though often earnest, were and must be consequently far from having a good and firm foundation on which to rest. But in the clearer light of the Christian revelation all is consistent, significant, and satisfactory. The deepest cravings of our nature are here met, and the

soul rests upon the word and promise of God as upon the basis of an everlasting rock.

2. Again we see the nature and necessity of making preparation for death and a future state. It is to believe in God and in the record which He has given of His Son, that if thou shalt confess with thy mouth the Lord Jesus, and shalt believe in thine heart that God hath raised him from the dead, thou shalt be saved. And this is the work of God, that ye believe in him whom He hath sent: and then it is added in another place, "Show me thy faith without thy works, and I will show thee my faith by my works; for faith without works is dead, being alone." Then since by nature we are alien from God, having rebelled against Him, doth not reason teach, as well as revelation declare, what is now so vitally enforced by our own experience even under human government and in this imperfect earthly state of society, that there must be repentance and regeneration of heart and reformation of life in order to the restoration of those who have so rebelled and so endeavored to destroy the government and disintegrate society itself? We cannot fail to see the reasonableness and the imperative motive of all this under the Divine government, however it may be questioned in those political systems which have been erected by the hands of men.

3. We may see also from the example before us the inheritance of a pious ancestry. They who consider the worth of things in their proper light will readily assent to this great truth, that there is a hereditariness of influence descending from generation to generation, which renders the character of our ancestry a matter of the deepest moment and concern to all their posterity. And on this point permit me to introduce the testimony of an old friend and college class-mate of the departed senator, which has just now been kindly furnished:

"When Solomon Foot was a member of college, he was living with a widowed mother, who had removed to Middlebury to give her son the peculiar literary and religious advantages that the place afforded. It was understood in the class that the father of Mr. Foot, a physician, I think, by profession, had been a man of very decided religious character; and this was judged to be a favorable circumstance by the religious members, when speculating on the probabilities of the son's conversion. The father was judged a man who must have derived great consolation, in his early separation from his family by death, from a scripture passage like this : 'Leave thy fatherless children ; I will preserve them alive, and let thy widows trust in me.'

" But the widowed mother of Mr. Foot is particularly remembered by her prevailing anxiety for his conversion and usefulness. I scarcely can recollect an interview that I had with that excellent lady, during my four years' residence at Middlebury, in which this was not the burden of her conversation. I have often thought that the mother of Augustine never felt more anxiety and persevering desire for her son's conversion than did the mother of Solomon Foot for his conversion."

4. We may see, too, the value of early religious training, and the benefit of an habitual observance of the ordinances of God's house. I have had occasion to observe many persons in the closing scenes of life, and I have never found one who had enjoyed such training and observed such habits that did not exhibit the fruit of it in the final hour. Nor did I ever see one who had gone through life without them that did not manifest a corresponding deficiency in sentiment, opinion, and experience, when the last trial came upon them. This result must necessarily follow ; and that human being who has come into and gone out of this life without such a training and such a habit deserves the most profound commiseration.

5. We may see, again, the consistency and dignity of a Christian life and the satisfaction of a Christian hope. Such a life bears in it a self-demonstrating power ; such a hope is evidence of its own priceless, inestimable nature. Those who have attained them in early years, and worn them well to a good old age, show by their example as well as their profession how true and how real is the excellency they possess. And those who have to regret their long neglect of or indifference to such a life and such a hope still bear witness to the incomparable value and desirableness of both. They are confirmed by a sense both of their loss and of their gain, both now and for evermore.

6. We see once more the beauty and glory of a Christian death and the abounding faithfulness of a covenant-keeping God. What clearness, calmness, composure, moral sublimity, in the chamber where a child of God is dying! How surely, tenderly, punctually is the Almighty power and grace vouchsafed to make "all that bed in peace," and to fill the dying scene with memorials the most living and the most lasting and the most affecting of all human experience on earth! And it is God's power and verity displayed when He says, "I will never leave thee nor forsake thee!" Oh, who in view of all this would not strive to lead this life, that our departure from it may be joyful and triumphant? And who would not exclaim with one of old and with a clearer motive, "Let me die the death of the righteous, and let my last end be like his?"

At the conclusion of Rev. Dr. Sunderland's eloquent discourse, during the delivery of which the immense audience was sensibly moved, Rev. Dr. Boynton, chaplain of the House of Representatives, offered a fervent prayer and pronounced the benediction.

———

The order of procession was then announced by Senator Doolittle, chairman of the committee of arrangements, as follows :

Chaplains of Congress for the occasion.

The Physicians who attended the Deceased.

Mr. Doolittle,				Mr. Hendricks,
Mr. Anthony,	}	Committee of Arrangements.	{	Mr. Sherman,
Mr. Howard.				Mr. Buckalew.
Mr. Fessenden,	}		{	Mr. Guthrie,
Mr. Harris,	}	Pall-bearers.	{	Mr. Lane, of Indiana,
Mr. Johnson,	}		{	Mr. Sumner.

THE CORPSE.

The Family and Friends of the Deceased.

The Senator and Representatives from the State of Vermont, as Mourners.

Citizens of the State of Vermont.
The Sergeant-at-arms of the Senate of the United States.
The members of the Senate, preceded by the President of the
Senate *pro tem.* and Secretary of the Senate.
The Acting Sergeant-at-arms of the House of Representatives.
The members of the House of Representatives, preceded
by its Speaker and Clerk.
The President of the United States.
The Heads of Departments.
The Diplomatic Corps.
Judges of the United States.
Officers of the Executive Departments.
Officers of the Army and Navy.
The Mayor of Washington.
Citizens and Strangers.

The procession moved through the rotundo of the Capitol, out of
the east door, and around the eastern grounds down to the depot of
the Baltimore and Ohio railroad. The next morning the corpse was
taken to Rutland, Vermont, escorted by Senators Poland, of Vermont; Doolittle, of Wisconsin; Ramsey, of Minnesota, and Riddle,
of Delaware, with the family and personal friends of the deceased;
attended by A. P. Gorman, Deputy Sergeant-at-arms of the Senate.

PROCEEDINGS AT RUTLAND, VERMONT.

Remarks of Messrs. POLAND *and* DOOLITTLE.

On the arrival of the remains of Mr. Foot at Rutland, Vermont, they were temporarily deposited in the United States court-house, which is in itself a monument to his memory, for it was mainly through his exertions that appropriations were passed for its erection, and in it he deposited his valuable law library.

In transferring the care of the remains from the senatorial committee to the committee of arrangements of the State of Vermont, Mr. POLAND said:

MR. CHAIRMAN AND FRIENDS: We come to you in the performance of a sad and melancholy duty. I come nominally as the chairman of a committee of the Senate of the United States, appointed to attend the remains of our deceased brother and your townsman and friend, the Hon. Solomon Foot, to his State and home. But the real character in which I come is that of one of his mourners, and I believe I can most truly say that aside from those closely connected to him by the ties of kindred, there is no one who more sincerely mourns his loss, or feels more deeply the bereavement caused by his death, than I do. The feeling of grief is too deep and personal to allow me to properly express myself upon this occasion, and I have therefore requested one of my colleagues of the committee, Senator Doolittle, of Wisconsin, to act as the organ of the committee in communicating our sad message to you.

MR. DOOLITTLE said:

MR. CHAIRMAN AND GENTLEMEN OF THE COMMITTEE: As my colleague upon the committee has truly said, we have come upon a sad errand. We have been commissioned by the Senate of the United States to bear home to Vermont all that is mortal of Solomon Foot. These remains, this precious dust, will now pass from our charge, as a committee of the Senate, to you, as representing the people of

his native State. It is no time or place for eulogy. Our hearts
are too full for that. A great sorrow has fallen upon the Senate,
and upon the whole country, as well as upon Vermont. That he
was distinguished as a statesman and senator all the world knows;
but what I desire to say, and what my heart most prompts me to say,
is, not that he was distinguished, honored, and respected, but that he
was beloved by every member of the Senate, of every political party.
All were his personal friends. Enemies he had none. The oldest
member of the body in continuous service, he was revered as the
father of the Senate. Often called upon to be its presiding officer,
and always watchful of its honor, he did more than any other to
preserve its dignity and decorum. But he has left the Senate. His
place we cannot fill. His like we may not look upon. Gentlemen,
here in that coffin is his lifeless body. We commit it to your charge.
Our mission in behalf of the Senate is fulfilled; our sad but sacred
office performed; our work done. We are now ready to return. But
I cannot take leave of you without saying that I am here in another
character, and, as the bearer of another message from him, as a dying
man, to you, the people of Rutland and Vermont. Bear in mind
that for more than eight years we had been in constant daily political
and friendly intercourse, a part of the time lodging under the same
roof, and most of the time sitting at the same table. He was to me
like a father or an elder brother. In these intimate relations I came
to know him well, and to love him more. But I did not know how
much I loved him, until standing at his bedside, the dying man
stretched out his hand, and clasping mine in his, said: "Dear brother,
you have always been kind to me—a dear, good brother senator. I
can never reward you; but you know where your reward lies"
I could not speak. But he continued in a clear and distinct voice,
while his face beamed with a heavenly light, to speak of the religion
of the Gospel, and of its consolations in sickness and in health.
Among other things, I remember he said: "The mercy of God has
been very great to me in this sickness. I have so many kind friends;
like so many angelic ministers all around me. It seems as though
a company of angels were all about me, to bear up my sinking

spirit." Then, after a pause, he said, "I have been trying to recall if there is any human being upon earth whom I have intentionally wronged or injured. I do not now remember any; but if there be any I pray that God will forgive me." I will not attempt to tell you all he said. Before I left the room, however, he said, in the same clear voice, to another: "The Lord reigns; let the earth rejoice! It is well that he does reign; and the people have reason to rejoice that he does reign. Yes, God reigns over all; there can be no doubt of that. We do not come into this world by mere chance; we are not creatures of accident. We are born to an eternal life." Here he paused a few moments, and then uttered that dying message, which I now bear to you. "When I leave this chamber," said he, "I wish no parade, no ostentatious demonstrations to be made; only the ordinary proceedings which custom and propriety impose; I desire to be borne to my friends and home in Rutland, Vermont—a people who have always been faithful to me—more faithful to me than I have been to them, I fear. They have done so much for me. I have no house there, but they will provide everything needful, and there, by them, among that people, let me be buried." This is the message which I bring to you from your dying friend. I was not present when he breathed his last; but from the account which I received immediately after from those who were present, his consciousness remained clear to the last, and his utterance distinct almost to the very last breath. In his last words, distinctly uttered, he left another message, which speaks not only to you and to me, but to all men, and for all time. In all history, I do not remember to have read of a dying Christian whose last words were more touching, more heavenly, and more triumphant over death and the grave. Seeing his time was at hand, the words of the twenty-third Psalm were then repeated to him by his wife. He called her to his side, folded his arms around her for a moment; then, as his breathing became more choked, he said: "What! Can this be death? So easy? Is it come already?" In a few moments after, with a face lighted up, as with a soul just entering into Paradise, he joyfully exclaimed: "I see it! I see it! The gates are wide open!

Beautiful! Beautiful!" And in a very few moments after uttering these words he expired. As a statesman and senator we honor him; as a man of noble character, we cherish his memory; as a true and faithful friend, we love him; as a dying Christian, what a glorious example has he left to all mankind!

Colonel W. T. NICHOLS, on behalf of the Committee of Arrangements, replied : Mr. Chairman and Senators : The people of Vermont, through a committee of the people of this town, accept the completion of the trust committed to your charge by the Senate of the United States, and receive at your hands the mortal remains of your distinguished colleague, and their honored and faithful representative. We receive what was mortal of our renowned and honored senator, our worthy citizen, our valued friend, as a sacred trust committed to our keeping. We receive the trust in sorrow, and will guard it tenderly. Your recital of the dying moments of the Hon. Solomon Foot fills our hearts too full for utterance in words. We mourn, and the people of Vermont are mourning to-day, at the loss of one of our greatest and best men. You have been pleased to allude to the high and honorable position occupied while living by him whose shrouded form lies before us. It is not fitting for me, at this hour and in this presence, to pronounce words of eulogy upon the character and public career of him who held for long years to this community the tenderer, the nearer and dearer relation than that of a trusted and distinguished representative in the highest branch of the national councils—the relation of a true and tried friend to the whole people; but in justice to his memory it may be said that the people of the State, which he honored by his services and his blameless life, were not indifferent observers, nor even unmindful that his usefulness, his name and fame, were national in extent; and, sir, while the honor of achieving such renown and influence was all his own, his State appropriated to itself an honest and unbounded pride in such a senator, and claimed his name and fame for Vermont. You have brought his remains from the halls of the American Senate chamber to the quiet retreat of his chosen home among the mountains of his native State, and communicated to us his dying message of gratitude to the people of his State and his home. We thank you, and through you tender our thanks and appreciation to the Senate who committed this trust to you. We assure you that if his colleagues had learned to love and to honor him in his older and riper years, the people who had known him earliest and longest honored and loved him best. And, sir, had there been any higher honor than a seat in that grand Areopagus of the American people—the Senate—the people of Vermont would have placed him in that higher position had it been in their power to do so. We take his mortal remains from your hands, and in the spot of his own choosing shall commit them to the earth—"dust to dust, and ashes to ashes ;" but while it will be tenderly, sacredly done, it will be done sorrowfully, mournfully, tearfully. That done, we will chisel the granite shaft, solid, plain, and simple, like his life and character, and strew his grave with the laurel and the cypress ; but in the respect and gratitude of the people of his home, a monument is already raised to his memory more enduring than the granite.

ADDRESSES

DEATH OF HON. SOLOMON FOOT.

IN THE SENATE OF THE UNITED STATES,
THURSDAY, APRIL 12, 1866.

Address of Mr. POLAND, of Vermont.

Mr. PRESIDENT: I offer the following resolutions:

Resolved, That the Secretary of the Senate be directed to inform the House of Representatives that the Senate, having listened to eulogies upon the character and public services of the Hon. SOLOMON FOOT, a senator from the State of Vermont, lately deceased, out of respect to his memory, have voted to adjourn.

Mr. President, two weeks ago this day it was my painful duty to announce to the Senate the death of my distinguished and beloved colleague, the Hon. SOLO-MON FOOT. The little time that elapsed between his decease and the funeral ceremonies here, and the absence of one of my colleagues of the House of Representatives, who was Mr. FOOT's immediate representative, were deemed sufficient reasons for postponing the customary obituary tributes to some future day. In accordance with the notice then given, I now ask that the Senate for a short time lay aside its ordinary business, and allow me and others the melancholy satisfaction of expressing our appreciation of the character, services, and virtues of our departed associate and friend. The last occasion of this kind in this chamber was early in the present session, in memory of my lamented predecessor. Judge Collamer. No one of us will ever forget the eloquent and loving words of Mr. Foot on that occasion in dwelling upon the memory of his long-time friend and colleague. As we looked at his robust and majestic form, and listened to his deep, rich voice and solemn, weighty words, how little we thought that in so short a time he, too, would have become only an object of memory and a subject of eulogy. Who next in this body of representatives of States shall be called from this high place to the unseen world? No one of us can tell. How solemnly are we reminded that death comes as a thief in the night, and how wisely are we cautioned, "Be ye also ready."

Mr. Foot was born in Cornwall, Addison county, Vermont, on the 19th day of November, 1802. I have not been able to learn anything in relation to his early life, but I infer that his family condition was such as to make all attainment and advancement in life depend upon his own efforts and labors. I infer this from the fact that he graduated from Middlebury college about 1826 or 1827, and somewhat later in life than is usual with young men where the means of education are provided by others. After his graduation he spent some time in teaching, and at the same time studying law. After his admission to the bar he commenced

practice in the town of Rutland, Vermont, and that
continued to be his place of residence up to the time
of his death.

He was elected a representative from the town of
Rutland to the Vermont house of representatives in
1833, 1836, 1837, and 1838, and again in the year 1847,
and during the last three of those years was speaker of
the house. He was a member of the State constitutional convention in 1836, which made the important
alteration in our State constitution of exchanging the
old legislative council for a State senate. He also held
the office of prosecuting attorney for Rutland county
from 1836 to 1842. In 1842 Mr. Foot was elected to
the lower house of Congress, and re-elected in 1844,
but declined further election. In 1850 he was elected
to the Senate of the United States, re-elected in 1856,
and again in 1862, and at the time of his death was the
oldest member in continuous service in this body.

Mr. Foot very soon attained a highly respectable
position as a lawyer. He was careful and attentive to
the interests of his clients, and always made full and
elaborate preparation for the trial of his causes. If his
life had been devoted to his profession, he would doubtless have attained high rank as a lawyer. But his
attention was early turned to political life, and his professional career was too broken and desultory to enable
him to attain the highest distinction in it. His ability
and character were far better suited to a public and
popular rather than a mere professional life. He had

been but a very few years at the bar, and a resident of the town of Rutland. when he was chosen to represent that town in the State legislature. It was quite rare at that day that so young a man was chosen to represent one of the oldest and most important towns in the State, and which contained many leading public men But he had already attained a high position as an able and popular speaker upon public and political questions, and his career in the State legislature added to this a reputation as a wise and careful legislator.

It was as speaker of the Vermont house of representatives that he first displayed that almost wonderful aptitude and capacity as the presiding officer of a deliberative assembly which afterwards made him so celebrated throughout the nation when he became the presiding officer of the Senate of the United States. as, perhaps, the best presiding officer in the whole country. He seemed almost to have been made for the position. His fine. majestic person. his dignified deportment, his full and rich voice. his easy and graceful manner. all conspired to make him a most useful and acceptable president over any assembly.   His knowledge of parliamentary law and usage was very thorough, but not more so. probably, than many others.   His superiority in this respect appeared born in him.   His look preserved order: the slightest word allayed confusion. The same grace of person and dignity of manner attended him always and everywhere, and was equally pleasing and agreeable in private society or on the

Senate floor. It had nothing of haughtiness or arrogance, but was kindly and benignant. It had doubtless much to do with the almost universal personal love and reverence felt for him by all who knew him.

Mr. Foot was not a man of great originality. I am not aware of any great public measure that he originated. He did not take much part in the debates in the Senate upon general subjects, but he was always in his seat, careful and watchful of all measures, with excellent judgment of what was for the public interest. A member of the present cabinet, who served ten years with him in the Senate, said to me during Mr. Foot's sickness, that he never knew a man whose votes were always more consistently right than his. When he did speak in the Senate, it was generally with careful preparation, and then he spoke wisely and well, and was listened to with great attention and respect. He was always faithful and prompt in his attendance on his committees, in making his reports, and in the performance of every public duty; but it was especially in his duty to his State, and the people of his State, that his watchfulness, energy, and untiring efforts were mainly directed. No interest of Vermont was allowed to suffer or remain unguarded, either in Congress or in any department of the general government. And so with every citizen of the State having right or claim or proper request upon any department of the government, Mr. Foot made it his own special duty to see it righted.

He loved and honored Vermont; he was proud that it was the place of his birth. More than once since I became his colleague he has mentioned the fact to me that never before was Vermont represented in the Senate by two of her sons born on her own soil, and he seemed to dwell on the idea with great satisfaction. During his illness, and after he became satisfied he should not recover, he loved to speak of being carried back to his native State; of being buried under the shadow of her grand mountains and green hills, and within sound of her waterfalls, and that his grave would be among his own people, whom he loved, and who loved him so well.

Mr. Foot's real greatness and the cause of his universal popularity I have not yet named. Some men are called great from a single great action—others by a few great deeds. Mr. Foot was a great man by reason of his great heart; not a single act or several acts of great statesmanship, but a lifetime of good and generous and unselfish deeds, made him great, and gave him such a hold upon the hearts of the people of his own State and others who knew him.

His mental faculties were of a high order; his acquirements were very respectable indeed; his judgment was excellent; he had extraordinary gifts of person and manners; but many men possessing all these in equal degree would never have attained a tithe of the honor and respect he did. It was his generous, warm-hearted love and sympathy for his fellows, and his

exhibition of it to them and for them at all times, that
induced their love and respect for him. You saw with
me the general exhibition of sorrow for his death here,
where he had been so long and was so well known and
so highly respected; but it was my fortune to be one
of your committee to attend his remains to his old
home and among the neighbors and associates of his
daily home life. Had you witnessed the deep gloom
and sadness that hung over that whole community, the
tears that filled so many eyes as we fulfilled our melancholy duty, you might well have exclaimed, "Behold
how they loved him!" Living in another part of the
State from Mr. Foot, and our pursuits for many years
having been so different, I had never much personal
intimacy with him until the commencement of the
present session, when I became his colleague. From
that time till his death we lived in the same house, and
till his sickness at the same table. I soon saw why all
loved and respected him, and shared their sentiments in
the fullest manner.

The infinite pains he took to make my position agreeable; to make me acquainted with the course and details
of business in the Senate; the proper offices and departments for everything—in short, the whole routine of congressional drudgery, which it is so important for every
man to know, and still every man is expected to find out
for himself—was what I did not expect from him, and
probably should have received from no other man. But
with his nature he could hardly have avoided doing it.

The circumstances of his sickness and death were such that general publicity has been given to various interviews and partings between him and valued friends, solemn and affecting in their character and interest I took my last leave of him on that same afternoon before his death. I could not now attempt to describe it, but I shall never forget his affectionate language or his solemn benediction at our parting.

I mourn his loss in common with all who knew him; but, with all who believe in the heaven hereafter, I doubt not that our loss is his infinite gain. His triumphant Christian death was a fitting end for so loving and useful a life.

Well may we all pray that our lives and our deaths may be like his. Sorely, indeed, has my native State been stricken; her two most distinguished sons, long her joint representatives in this body, where they represented her with so much ability, usefulness, and credit, both taken away by death, and so near each other that the stunning effect of the first blow had hardly passed when the other came. God grant that those who have survived and succeeded them may be enabled in some degree to emulate their virtues and usefulness to the State and people thus bereaved!

Address of Mr. JOHNSON, *of Maryland.*

Mr. PRESIDENT: I rise briefly to participate in paying honor to the memory of our departed friend and associate. Such tributes to virtues, public and private, as he possessed, cannot fail to benefit the living as well as honor the dead. They show those who are commencing life how it is, and what it is, to earn a name that will live after death, and be to family and friends a priceless heritage. They show the value of honest fame, a fame which survives death, and becomes brighter as time rolls on. They show how immeasurably superior in the estimation of the good is such fame to that sickly evanescent one which is occasionally achieved by artful and dishonorable contrivances.

The life, too, of a Christian man, as SOLOMON FOOT was, if no other evidence existed of the truth of the Christian dispensation, would be sufficient to demonstrate it. Its influence upon him in this world, its comfort, its joy to him in death, is sufficient to establish its divine origin. He who with evident sincerity, and while his mind was as perfect as ever, nearly at the moment of dissolution, could say that he felt "borne up as on angels' wings," and in the very moment preceding it, with hand and eyes uplifted, could exclaim, "I see it! I see it! The gates are wide open! Beautiful! Beautiful!" and then die, is a witness to our faith that the sophistries of skepticism can never counteract.

The memory of such a man should not be lost. It is not enough that it may survive in the recollection of his family and friends; it should live in the records of the body to which he was so long attached, and which he so faithfully served and honored. The Senate of the United States should perpetuate the evidence that SOLOMON FOOT was for years one of its most honored members, respected, admired, loved by every associate for his faithfulness, his patriotism, his endearing social qualities, and revered for his Christian death. This will be done by the proceedings of this day.

Mr. Foot's public career is now so well known that it would be idle in me to attempt its detail. This has been done by his colleague. Seldom engaging in debate, we yet knew, in advance, the result to which his sound judgment, ever unswayed by passion or prejudice, would lead him. Though in a large and comprehensive sense a party man, his principles were adopted because they, in his estimation, led to general and not partial good. No sectional feeling ever consciously influenced him. His mind and his heart embraced his whole country, and he loved even his native Vermont, to which he was so strongly attached, the more because it was a part of the great whole. His reading, his familiarity with the history of his country, his experience had convinced him that national prosperity and renown, as well as the happiness of the several States, could only be attained through the Union established by our fathers, and he could never, therefore, tolerate

those who threatened its dissolution or foolishly
attempted, with a view to depreciate it, to calculate its
value. In heart and mind a Unionist, he entered zeal-
ously into all the measures calculated to terminate our
recent civil strife; and although in some respects, I
believe, not a very sanguine man, he never doubted a
successful result. It was encouraging to hear him
speak on the subject. He had studied our institutions,
had become extensively acquainted with our people,
and knew how deep was their attachment to the general government; and with this knowledge he was
satisfied that the first were adequate to meet the emer-
gency if their powers were exerted, and that the latter
would peril all to have them exerted. He lived, thank
God, to see his prediction verified. When he left us
he knew that the strife was over, the Union everywhere
reinstated in all its rightful authority, and that nothing
remained to be done but by proper efforts to calm the
agitation inseparable from such a contest, and win us
all back into our ancient brotherhood.

Mr. President, although we shall no more see our late
brother in this chamber, which of us will ever forget
his manly presence, his uniform dignity, his ever constant watchfulness over the proper decorum of the
body, his unbending firmness, his uniform courtesy as
its frequent presiding officer! And, above all, which
of us who listened to the touching story of his last days
on earth, as recently told us by the reverend clergyman
who was his pastor in this city, but will have cause to

rejoice if he can live and die as lived and died SOLOMON
FOOT—dying, to use his own truthful words in his
eulogy on his former colleague, Jacob Collamer, so
affectingly delivered in this chamber on the 14th of
December last, and so strikingly applicable to himself—
"in the full exercise of his intellectual faculties, with
an abiding and unshaken faith in the Christian religion,
and in the cherished hope of a blissful immortality!"

Address of Mr. FESSENDEN, of Maine.

MR. PRESIDENT: In attempting to speak of one so
long associated with us, and endeared to us by so many
rare and excellent qualities, as the late Senator Foot, I
cannot but feel impressed with the difficulty of doing
perfect justice either to the man or the occasion; a
difficulty increased by the long, uninterrupted, almost
brotherly, friendship which existed between him and
myself. But, difficult as the task may be, I cannot, if
I would, withhold my tribute to the character and
memory of one so much beloved, and who is held by
all his associates in most affectionate remembrance.

The death of our friend was so unlooked for, his
promise of prolonged life and continued usefulness
seemed so secure, it is hard to realize that his place is
vacant, and that we shall see him no more upon earth.
But yesterday he stood among us, imposing in the

beauty and stateliness of perfect manhood, his face beaming with kindliness, his whole aspect dignified and serene, glowing with health and vigor; to-day all that was mortal of our friend and brother reposes in a distant grave, among those by whom he was loved, and trusted, and honored—a grave watered by many tears, and venerated for its sacred dust—while the true and noble spirit which once animated that clay has ascended to give an account of its mission upon earth, and to enjoy, as we may well believe, the reward of a well-spent life.

An event like this, touching in its significance, becomes the more startling when following closely upon another scarcely less impressive. In a single session of the Senate, within a few short months, we hear the announcement that Death has laid his icy fingers upon both senators from one of the States of this Union, each a man of eminent mark in this body, and at a period when the loss of their wisdom, their experience, their patriotism, their unswerving integrity, and unselfish devotion to their country's good, is most severely felt. That State has many noble and most worthy sons among whom it may choose for places of trust and honor; but no State can give at once to the public councils the assurance, which time only can bestow, of that fitness which experience and trial alone can prove and secure.

When, Mr. President, a man, however eminent in other pursuits, and whatever claims he may have to public confidence, becomes a member of this body, he has much to learn and much to endure. Little does he know of what he will have to encounter. He may be well read in public affairs, but he is unaware of the difficulties which must attend and embarrass every effort to render what he may know available and useful. He may be upright in purpose and strong in the belief in his own integrity, but he cannot even dream of the ordeal to which he cannot fail to be exposed; of how much courage he must possess to resist the temptations which daily beset him; of that sensitive shrinking from undeserved censure which he must learn to control; of the ever-recurring contest between a natural desire for public approbation and a sense of public duty; of the load of injustice he must be content to bear, even from those who should be his friends; the imputations on his motives; the sneers and sarcasms of ignorance and malice; all the manifold injuries which partisan or private malignity, disappointed of its object, may shower upon his unprotected head. All this, if he would retain his integrity, he must learn to bear unmoved, and walk steadily onward in the path of public duty, sustained only by the reflection that time may do him justice, or, if not, that his individual hopes and aspirations, and even his name among men, should be of little account to him when weighed in the balance against the welfare of a people, of whose destiny he is a constituted guardian and defender.

To such an ordeal, Mr. President, our lamented

friend was subjected for fourteen years, at a most trying period, and admirably did he bear the trial. Coming to the Senate when two antagonist forces had proclaimed what soon proved to be a hollow truce, he was a witness to the outbreak which marked its termination, and was a party to the struggle which, after several years, eventuated in civil war. From the first moment his course was clearly defined. Representing a people of strong convictions, and himself a child of free institutions, he could not but become their champion. Assuming no leadership, content to follow so long as the measures proposed commended themselves to his judgment and his conscience, his firm and vigorous support was always to be relied on as a certainty. He was not one to make capital for himself at the expense of his country, or of those with whom he acted. If work was to be done, he was ready to do it. If a trying moment came, it found him prepared. Whatever of dire portents might shoot across the political sky, with unshrinking heart he stood erect to meet, and, if possible, to avert, the threatened calamity. Deeply lamenting the terrible issue, sad and sometimes almost despairing as he witnessed its sanguinary results, there was no moment of doubt, not even of hesitation, with him. Let us rejoice and be thankful that he lived to see the dawn of a brighter day.

Through all this long period of fourteen years, checkered as they were with great events, the course of ordinary legislation has required a high degree of intellectual power. In a country like ours, where progress is so rapid, change so instantaneous, the human mind so active, new fields of effort so broad and diversified, legislation must accommodate itself to the necessities, and often to the impulse, of the hour. It is impossible here to travel steadily in ancient ways. The legislator who stands still will not meet the requirements of our day.

Of such our friend was not one. With an intellect broad and powerful in its grasp and enlarged by study and reflection, limited by no narrow or sectional views, just and liberal in spirit, looking upon his country as a whole, and loving it in all its parts, nothing that could aid in its development or advance its best interests failed to receive his sympathy and support. And seldom was his deliberate judgment at fault. To say that he might not sometimes have erred would be to proclaim him more than human. To assert that he was never wilfully wrong, or erred but where wise and good men might well differ, is doing him no more than justice. The crowning beauty of his public life, more than all else, was that whatever he did, however he might act, no spot was left upon the perfect enamel of his character as a legislator. Malice could not stain its whiteness. In all that he did there was that transparent truthfulness which attracts and secures the confidence of friends, and compels the respect, and even admiration, of adversaries—enemies, he had none

A stranger, Mr. President, upon entering this cham-

ber and casting his eyes around upon the Senate, could
not but be struck with the imposing presence of our
departed friend and associate, and attracted by the rare
union of mildness and dignity in his expressive features.
If he rose to speak, the commanding, yet pleasant,
tones of his voice, and the noble grace of his demeanor,
the elegance of his language, and his clear and forcible
statement, would deepen the first favorable impression.
If called to the chair, as he was more often than any
other, that seemed to be the place he was made to fill.
There was exhibited his remarkable love of order, his
impartiality, his sense of senatorial propriety, his entire
fitness to preside over and control the deliberations of
what should be a grave, decorous, and dignified body of
thoughtful men charged with great trusts, and alive to
their importance. Whatever was in the least degree
unbecoming was offensive to his feelings and his taste;
but however these might be offended, he never for a
moment forgot what was due to the Senate and to himself, as its officer. Would that his precepts and his
example in these particulars may not be forgotten.
Often, sir, when we look upon the chair you occupy,
however ably and faithfully it may be filled, must we
think of him whose admonitions we well remember,
and to whose unshaken firmness and unwearied patience
we were so often indebted for the preservation of that
respect which we owe to ourselves.

Averse to much speaking, Mr. Foot did not often
address the Senate, and never but after careful thought;

and yet he possessed every advantage for distinguished
success. His mental powers, as I have before remarked,
were carefully trained and cultivated, his command of
language was excellent, his taste correct, his voice so-
norous, and his action at once graceful and dignified.
That with such advantages he should have taken so
small a share in debate, especially in later years, when
he had become familiar with public affairs, must seem
not a little singular to those not acquainted with his
habits of thought and his peculiar temperament.   The
explanation, however, is simple, and may be found in
his remarkable want of self-appreciation.   Modest to a
fault, he never did anything like justice to his own
powers.   To others, and especially to those who possessed his confidence and affection, he did more than
justice, being too ready always to receive and defer to
the opinions of others in no respect superior to himself.
Thence it followed that he seldom addressed the Senate
upon subjects which occasioned general debate.   Upon
those rare occasions when his voice was heard, the questions were such, for the most part, as in his opinion had
not received the attention their importance deserved.
We all know the respect with which he was invariably
listened to, and the light shed by his intellect and his
industry upon whatever subject he chose to touch.

His political friends are well aware how this want of
self-assertion in merely personal matters was exhibited
in all his relations to and intercourse with them.
Though long the oldest member of the Senate in con-

secutive service, he invariably avoided conspicuous place. While others might seek for and claim desirable positions upon leading committees as due to their States, if not to themselves, he was satisfied with any that was assigned to him. however derogatory it might seem to his age and standing. preferring and urging the claims of others, and desiring only that all should be satisfied. Often have I known him to insist that his name should be struck from an important committee. in order to replace it with the name of a friend or associate to whom he thought the distinction would be grateful. To him more than any other was assigned the unenviable task of arranging these committees, not only because all confided in his sense of justice. but because of his disinterested magnanimity. I have often thought that such generous abnegation of self should not have been permitted. I know that on several occasions it was peremptorily overruled.

That such a senator, so useful, so modest, so unassuming, so courteous, so kind, of a deportment so unexceptionable, should have won the good-will of all his associates and the love of many, and that his loss should occasion universal sorrow, may well be supposed. Those, however, who saw and marked the crowds assembled to witness the last sad ceremonies, and who noted the many weeping eyes which looked upon his coffin, would naturally be led to consider that nothing in the routine of his public career could account for a grief so deep and so general. Men are not apt to be

mourned with tears for public services, or even on account of public or private virtue. Great intellectual
pre-eminence may excite admiration, but when the
light goes out its absence occasions but a weak and
transient emotion. Gifts and qualities like these "come
not near the heart." The secret of all that genuine and
unaffected sorrow for the friend we have lost lies in the
feeling of all who came within his sphere, that his was
a true and noble and loving nature: Impulsive and
ardent in temperament, he was kind, generous, and for-
giving. If injury excited him to anger, it was a generous anger which could hardly outlive the occasion, and
perished of itself if let alone. Enthusiastic in his friendship, no labor was too severe, no sacrifice too great, for
those to whom he gave his affection. He was proud of
his country, of his State, of his friends. For himself
he was humble. Of an open hand, his charity was
instantaneous and unsuspecting. If

> "He prayeth best who loveth best
> All things, both great and small,"

then was he a man of prayer. And if "the chamber
where a good man meets his fate" is holy, then may we
rejoice who were permitted to feel the loveliness of his
dying hour.

Admirable senator! patriotic citizen! good and true
man! dear and cherished friend! this scene of your
many labors will know you no more, but long will your
memory dwell in these halls! This marble pile, bear-

ing the impress of your watchful care, is one of your
monuments. Its massive pillars will stand erect, giving
their testimony to our country's grandeur long, long
after we and generations yet to come shall have passed
like shadows upon the water; yet he who, like yourself,
shall have performed his duty in life, and died with a
Christian's hope, will survive when all these columns
shall be lost to sight in the accumulated dust of ages.

Address of Mr. BROWN, of Missouri.

Mr. PRESIDENT: When it was signified that a subsequent day would be set apart for appropriate commemoration in honor of the lately deceased senator from
Vermont, I had designed preparing some extended
tribute to attest my warm regard for his virtues and
my great appreciation of his talents. An indisposition,
however, that has prostrated me almost to the present
moment, will prevent my doing as I would have wished.
Still I am not willing to let this occasion pass without
any memorial word from my lips.

Long years ago, sir, I learned to admire the steadfast
devotion to free principles, amid the thick conflict of
impending revolution, manifested in the public life of
Senator FOOT. There was a moral force, an undemon-
strative heroism, in his quiet methods of persistence,
impressive far beyond any pronounced mannerism.

But it was only when I came to know him personally
in the relations of private intercourse that I realized
the force and beauty of his full-orbed manhood.

The reciprocal action of thought and feeling so often
dissociated by the wear of political avocation was with
him a perfect accord. Among the first who extended
to me the hand of welcome upon my entrance into this
body, he emphasized that welcome by a cordial manner, a refined courtesy, an unselfish guidance, and from
that hour until the hour of his departure I can truly
say that I relied upon his friendship with a confidence
as absolute as if it had been the growth of years. It
seemed as though the animation of his noble nature
shone out radiant from his person; that a countenance
in which was blended boldness and sweetness gave true
index of the spirit within. And such as he seemed I
ever found him to be—a man free from guile, pure in
patriotism, clear of faith, upright, punctual, deliberate,
and wise with the wisdom that comes of observation,
which develops in action rather than argument, and
which is serene because it is ever charitable.

Of a large type of intellect, capable of most moving
speech, graceful beyond most in elocution, he was seldom heard in the debates of this chamber, and yet it
will be said of him that few, if any, better fulfilled the
proper duties of a senator, or did more thoroughly the
work assigned him, either by constituents or compeers.
Often chosen to preside here, eminently worthy of such
dignity, possessed with a voice rich in melody, quick of

apprehension amid diverse questioning, rapid in judg-ments, yet modest in affirmation, he became at last the oracle of the Senate, to whom all referred in disputed matters of parliamentary ruling. Observant, scrupu-lously observant, of the forms and ceremonies that usage has grown, like mosses, around the procedure of this the most august deliberative body of the world, he was yet even more deferential to duty than to form or cere-mony. Indeed, I think if he had one dominant element that ruled all else in his evenly balanced mind, it was a rigid, unswerving sense of duty that would suffer no consideration to set aside its claim; a sense of duty to which, in the prime of a vigorous physical development, he, by too assiduous devotion, sacrificed his life.

But why do I say sacrificed his life? Has he not gone rather to the eternal life beyond those "beautiful gates" which shone upon his fading vision with un-earthly splendor, into the everlasting tabernacles of light and love, to dwell forever with his God? Stand-ing by the side of that dying statesman, witnessing with what composure he consciously drew near his dissolution; hearing him pronounce the vanity and emptiness of titled honors when present with death, and yet kindle into exultation and triumph as he spoke of his infinite hope in a redeemed resurrection; humbly partaking with him of that last sacrament that sealed him to the church, and bidding him a farewell, full of sympathy to me, full of joy to him, I cannot think we have any right to mourn here to-day.

Let us, then, Mr. President, cherish the example of that life which he led as worthy to be our guide in performing those high trusts committed to our charge, and let us deal with the memory of him who has passed from our midst, not as a memory draped with the signs of mourning, but bright and beautiful and glorious, fit to be crowned with music and with flowers, not with elegiac responses.

Address of Mr. SUMNER, of Massachusetts.

Mr. PRESIDENT: There is a truce in this chamber. The antagonism of debate is hushed. The echoes of conflict have died away. The white flag is flying. From opposite camps we come together to bury the dead. It is a senator that we bury, and not a soldier.

This is the second time during the present session that we have been called to mourn a distinguished senator from Vermont. It was much to bear such a loss once. Its renewal now after so brief a period is a calamity without precedent in the history of the Senate. No State before has ever lost two senators so near together.

Mr. FOOT at his death was the oldest senator in continuous service. He entered the Senate in the same Congress with the senator from Ohio (Mr. WADE) and myself; but he was sworn in at the called session in

March, while the two others were not sworn in till the
succeeding December.   During this considerable space
of time I have been the constant witness to his life and
conversation.   It is with a sentiment of gratitude that
I look back upon our relations, never from the beginning impaired or darkened by any difference.   For one
brief moment he seemed disturbed by something that
fell from me in the unconscious intensity of my convictions, but it was for a brief moment only, and he took
my hand with a genial grasp.   I make haste also to
declare my sense of his personal purity and his incorruptible nature.   Such elements of character, exhibited
and proved throughout a long service, render him an
example for all.   He is gone, but these virtues "smell
sweet and blossom in the dust."

He was excellent in judgment.   He was excellent
also in speech, so that whenever he spoke the wonder
was that he who spoke so well should speak so rarely.
He was full, clear, direct, emphatic, and never was
diverted from the thread of his argument.   Had he
been moved to mingle actively in debate, he must have
exerted a commanding influence over opinion in the
Senate and in the country.   How often we have
watched him tranquil in his seat while others, without
his experience or weight, occupied attention.   The
reticence which was a part of his nature formed a contrast to that prevailing effusion where sometimes the
facility of speech is less remarkable than the inability
to keep silent; and, again, it formed a contrast to that

controversial spirit which too often, like an unwelcome
wind, puts out the lights, while it fans a flame. And
yet in his treatment of questions he was never incom-
plete or perfunctory. If he did not say, with the orator
and parliamentarian of France, the famous founder of
the *Doctrinaire* school of politics, M. Royer Collard,
that he had too much respect for his audience ever to
ask attention to anything which he had not first
written, it was evident that he never spoke in the
Senate without careful preparation. You do not forget
his commemoration of his late colleague only a few
short weeks ago, when he delivered a funeral oration
not unworthy of the French school from which this
form of eloquence is derived. Alas! as we listened to
that most elaborate eulogy, shaped by study and pene-
trated by feeling, how little did we think that it was so
soon to be echoed back from his own tomb!

It was not in our debates only that this self-abnega-
tion showed itself. He quietly withdrew from places
of importance on committees to which he was entitled,
and which he would have filled with honor. More
than once I have known him to insist that another
should take the position assigned to himself. He was
far from that nature which Lord Bacon exposes, in pun-
gent humor, when he speaks of "extreme self-lovers,
who would burn a house in order to roast their eggs."
And yet it must not be disguised that he was happy in
the office of senator. It was to him as much as his
"dukedom" to Prospero. He felt its honors and con-

fessed its duties. But he was content. He desired nothing more. Perhaps no person appreciated so thoroughly what it was to bear the commission of a State in this chamber. Surely no person appreciated so thoroughly all the dignities which belong to the Senate. Of its ceremonial he was the admitted arbiter.

There was no jealousy, envy, or uncharitableness in him. He enjoyed what others did, and praised generously. He knew that his own just position could not be disturbed by the success of another. Whatever another may be, whether more or less, a man must always be himself. A true man is a positive, and not a relative, quantity. Properly inspired, he will know that in a just sense nobody can stand in the way of another. And here let me add that, in proportion as this truth enters into practical life, we shall all become associates and coadjutors rather than rivals. How plain that, in the infinite diversity of character and talent, there is a place for every one. This world is wide enough for all its inhabitants; this republic is grand enough for all its people. Let every one serve in his place according to the faculties that have been given to him.

In the long warfare with slavery Mr. FOOT was from the beginning firmly and constantly on the side of freedom. He was against the deadly compromises of 1850. He linked his shield in the small, but solid, phalanx of the Senate which opposed the Nebraska bill. He was faithful in the defence of Kansas, menaced by slavery.

And when at last this barbarous rebel took up arms, he accepted the issue, and did all that he could for his country. But even the cause which for years he had so much at heart did not lead him into debate, except very rarely. His opinions appeared in votes rather than in speeches. But his sympathies were easily known. I do not forget that when I first came into the Senate, and was not yet personally familiar with him, I was assured by Mr. Giddings, who knew him well, that he belonged to the small circle who would stand by freedom, and the anti-slavery patriarch added pleasantly that Mr. Foot, on his earliest visit to the House of Representatives after he became senator, drew attention by coming directly to his seat and sitting by his side in friendly conversation. Mr. Foot by the side of Joshua R. Giddings, in those days when slavery still tyrannized, is a picture not to be forgotten. If our departed friend is not to be named among those who have borne the burden of this great controversy, he must not be forgotten among those whose sympathies with liberty never failed. Would that he had done more. Let us be thankful that he did so much.

There is a part on the stage known as the "walking gentleman," who has very little to say, but who always appears well. Mr. Foot might seem, at times, to have adopted this part, if we were not constantly reminded of his watchfulness in everything concerning the course of business, and the administration of parliamentary law. Here he excelled and was the master of us all.

The division of labor, which is the lesson of political
economy, is also the lesson of public life. All cannot
do all things. Some do one thing; others do another
thing; each according to his gifts. This diversity pro-
duces harmony.

The office of President *pro tempore* among us grows
out of the anomalous relations of the Vice-President
to the Senate. There is no such officer in the other
house, nor was there in the House of Commons until
very recently, when we read of a "deputy speaker,"
which is the term by which he is addressed when in
the chair. No ordinary talent can guide and control a
legislative assembly, especially if it be numerous, or if it
be excited by party differences. A good presiding
officer is like Alexander mounting Bucephalus. The
assembly knows its master "as a horse knows its rider."
This was pre-eminently the case of Mr. Foot, who was
often in the chair, and was for a considerable period
our President *pro tempore*. Here he showed a special
adaptation and power. He was in person "every inch"
a President; so also was he in every sound of the voice.
He carried into the chair the most marked individuality
that has been seen there during this generation. He
was unlike any other presiding officer. None but himself could be his parallel. His presence was felt in-
stantly. It filled this chamber from floor to gallery.
It attached itself to everything that was done. Vigor
and despatch prevailed. Questions were stated so as
to challenge attention. Impartial justice was manifest

at once. Business in every form was handled with
equal ease. Order was enforced with no timorous
authority. If disturbance came from the gallery, how
promptly he launched his fulmination. If it came from
the floor, you have seen him throw himself back, and
then, with voice of lordship, as if all the Senate was
in him, insist that debate should be suspended until
order was restored. "The Senate must come to order,"
he exclaimed, while, in unison with his powerful voice,
he beat with ivory hammer, like another god Thor,
until the reverberations rattled like thunder in the
mountains.

The Duke de Morny, who was the accomplished
president of the legislative assembly of France, in a
sitting shortly before his death, after sounding his
crier's bell, which is the substitute for the hammer
among us, exclaimed from the chair, "I shall be obliged
to mention by name the members whom I find con-
versing. I declare to you that I shall do so, and I shall
have it put in the Moniteur. You are here to discuss
and to listen, not to converse. I promise you that I
will do what I say to the very first I catch talking."
Possibly our President might have found occasion for a
similar speech, but his energy in the enforcement of
order stopped short of this menace. Certainly he did
everything consistent with the temper of the Senate,
and he showed always what Sir William Scott, on one
occasion in the House of Commons, placed among the
essential qualities of a speaker, when he said that "to

a jealous affection for the privileges of the House
must be added an awful sense of its duties."

Accustomed as we have become to the rules which
govern legislative proceedings, we are hardly aware of
their importance in the development of liberal institutions. They were unknown in antiquity, and they
were unknown also on the European continent until
latterly introduced from England, which was their
original home. They are among the precious contribu-
tions which England has made to modern civilization.
And yet they did not assume at once their present perfect form. Mr. Hallam tells us that even as late as
Queen Elizabeth members called confusedly for the
business they wished brought forward. But now, at
last, these rules have become a beautiful machine by
which business is conducted, legislation is moulded, and
debate is secured in all possible freedom. From the
presentation of a petition or the introduction of a bill
all proceeds by fixed processes until, without disorder,
the final result is reached, and a new law takes its place
in the statute-book. Hoe's printing-press or Alden's
type-setter is not more perfect in its operations. But
the rules are more even than a beautiful machine; they
are the very temple of constitutional liberty. In this
temple our departed friend served to the end with
pious care. His associates, as they recall his stately
form, silvered by time, but beaming with goodness, will
not cease to cherish the memory of this service. His
image will rise before them as the faithful presiding

officer by whom the dignity of the Senate was maintained, its business was advanced, and parliamentary
law was upheld.

He had always looked with delight upon this Capitol—one of the most remarkable edifices of the world—
beautiful in itself, but more beautiful still as the emblem of that national unity which he loved so well.
He enjoyed its enlargement and improvement. He
watched with pride its marble columns as they moved
into place, and its dome as it ascended to the skies.
Even the trials of the war did not make him forget it.
His care secured those appropriations by which the
work was carried to its close, and the statue of Liberty
was installed on its sublime pedestal. It was natural
that in his last moments, as life was failing fast, he
should long to rest his eyes upon an object which was
to him so dear. The early light of morning had come,
and he was lifted in his bed that he might once more
behold this Capitol with mortal sight; but there was
another capitol which already began to fill his vision,
fairer than your marble columns, sublimer than your
dome, where liberty without any statue is glorified in
that service which is perfect freedom.

Address of Mr. POMEROY, of Kansas.

Mr. PRESIDENT: I bring to the offerings of this occasion a grateful memory of the services rendered a struggling people in a distant Territory by the late Senator FOOT, of Vermont. Generous efforts made at a crisis in one's history can never be forgotten; and when such offerings are unsought and unrewarded they deserve honorable mention. I remember to have looked in upon the Senate of the United States when the affairs of the Territory of which I was a resident engaged the attention of Congress and the country. The period to which I refer was the 9th day of August, 1856. A few only of the distinguished members of the present session were then in this body. It was in the old Senate chamber, and the leaders in the debate on that day are now and have been for some years away from us. On the day previous the present presiding officer of this body had made for Kansas a most earnest, faithful, and eloquent speech. And I shall never forget the hour which the late senator from Vermont devoted to pleading the cause of our struggling people. I am sorry that speech has not been preserved. The Congressional Globe of that date says: "The speech will appear in the Appendix." I have searched the Appendix in vain, and I think it is not there. The only record of that memorable speech that I can find is contained in the National Intelligencer of the 11th of August, 1856, as follows:

"Mr. Foot rose to address the Senate for the first time, we believe, upon the Kansas troubles, which, sifted and discussed as that subject has been for months—and exhausted, were it possible—derived fresh interest from the ability, eloquence, and impressiveness with which it was treated by the honorable senator from Vermont. This luminous effort we hope to lay before our readers at an early day."—*Intelligencer, August* 11, 1856.

This is most invaluable testimony, as it comes from a source which did not then or now sympathize with the cause which was so ably vindicated. I remember well the eloquent and stirring appeal he made in our behalf. He demanded for us the rights of freemen under the Constitution—of free homesteads, free ballots, and a free State. Noble words, and "fitly spoken." They made an impression upon my own mind as indellible as the teaching of my boyhood, and I shall forget them only when I cease to remember any of the events of this .life; and not to recognize services rendered at such a crisis would be ingratitude which could not be pardoned; and far away beyond the valleys of the Mississippi and the Missouri there are quiet cabin homes where the name of SOLOMON FOOT is a household word. In the name of that people who cherish the memories of their benefactors with undying gratitude, I bring to-day this humble tribute of grateful acknowledgments. While others lay costlier and more imposing offerings upon his burial place, I will content myself by planting but a single shrub. It shall be an evergreen, for it is the unfading tribute of gratitude. "He opened his

mouth for the dumb," and did not shut his ear to the
cry of the poor: "and the cause that he knew not he
searched out." Such efforts, nobly rendered, shall not
be forgotten, for the people whom he vindicated were
not his people. They were separated from him by the
breadth of half the continent. But the cause which he
pleaded was the cause of freedom, the cause of his
countrymen—aye, the cause of mankind. For when one
member suffers all suffer; when one is degraded all are
dishonored.

> "Whatever link you strike"

from the great chain which binds the human family to
each other and to God,

> "Tenth or ten-thousandth,
> You break the chain alike."

Mr. President, the departed senator is not dead. No
man who has nobly lived can ever wholly die. The
deeds of good men live forever! their memory is
undying; and their influence is reflected by those who
live after them; and it lives on in endless circles.
widening and deepening forever and forever more.
Good men are reproduced in each generation, and their
lives are as immortal as truth, virtue, and God. Sir,
amidst the green hills and budding forests of the early
spring-time the senator sleeps, beloved, honored. and
embalmed even in the affections of his devoted home
circle of friends. But, sir, far away, across the wide
continent there are those who will hold him in per-

petual and grateful remembrance; and year by year,
as the seasons come and go, will a generous people, with offerings of gratitude, consecrate their little
children by giving them at the altar of their baptism
the honored name of the Senator who vindicated their
rights and secured them their liberties. But from this
burial scene we must tear ourselves away, for life has
its duties as well as death its lessons. We should not
yield to sorrow, for life, and death, even, have their
hopes. "For if a man die, he shall live again."
"When the heavens are no more he shall awake and
be raised out of his sleep."

> "Life is struggle, combat, victory;
>   Wherefore have we slumbered on
> With our forces all unmarshalled,
>   With our weapons all undrawn?
>
> "Oh, what a glorious record
>   Had the angels of me kept,
> If I'd done instead of doubted,
>   Had I warred instead of wept.
>
> "Build thy great acts high and higher,
>   Build them on the conquered sod,
> Where thy weakness first fell bleeding,
>   Where thy first prayer rose to God."

Address of Mr. CRAGIN, *of New Hampshire.*

Mr. PRESIDENT: Love for my native State, sympathy with her people in their double affliction, and great respect for the character of her departed senators, prompt me to utter a few words on this solemn occasion. Few members of the Senate have known SOLOMON FOOT longer than I have. Running back into the years of my boyhood is the memory of this able, pure, and accomplished man. More than thirty years ago I looked with pride and admiration upon his noble and manly form, and eagerly listened to his eloquent words. It was my fortune to have been born and reared within thirty miles of where both the late senators of Vermont long resided, and I can truly say that my political faith was in part derived from their teachings. Judge Collamer resided in my native county, and my first vote for member of Congress was given for him. Only a few weeks ago the death of that great and good man was fittingly announced in this chamber by his distinguished colleague, whose departure we now deplore. What we do for the dead must soon be done for us. In his concluding remarks on that occasion he seems to have had a presentiment that his own remaining days upon the earth would be few. He said:

"Mr. President, he whose death we now lament is gone, to be with us no more. His work on earth is done; he strikes a golden harp among the seraphim on high. His precepts and his example are left to us for our instruction and our profit. Happy, indeed, will it be if we shall so profit by them that we shall be ready, as he was ready, for the final summons in that hour which is coming to us all, and to some of us not far off, when this world and its worthlessness shall fade from our sinking vision."

These solemn words may now be spoken of him who first uttered them, and again to us. Surely, this life is short, very short. Man is here to-day, and gone to-morrow! He is as the transient grass: "in the morning it springeth up and flourisheth; in the evening it is cut down and withereth." The great highway of life is thronged; some are constantly falling in the race, and others are coming to take their places; and the world moves on as before, passing, generation after generation, into the awful shadow which no eye, except that of faith, can penetrate.

It is not my purpose to speak of the public career of our lamented friend, but simply to draw attention to his general character, and the example of his life. His social, moral, and mental qualifications were well adapted for use, and also for show. Of fine, commanding personal appearance, he always bore himself with great urbanity and dignity of manner. He was one of nature's noblemen. His features, his proportions, his manners, his mind, all indicated a man. God set the seal of greatness upon his brow, and planted within the elements of goodness and loving kindness. His was a heart of honor, and a tongue of truth. He was strong in his convictions, and bold in their utterance. He was a firm advocate for freedom and human rights,

and a most devoted lover of the republic. He was one
of the most perfect models of integrity and propriety
that I ever knew. Honor with him was a cardinal
virtue, and he had a most perfect taste for forms and
ceremonies. He abhorred meanness, scorned duplicity,
and despised trickery. In his case there was no pov-
erty of soul. He always looked and acted the perfect
man. The mantle of truth, which is the garment of
beauty and exalted manhood, he always wore. He was
a sound, practical, and learned man. Twenty-five years
ago he was a fluent and captivating speaker; but even
then his candor, truthfulness, and facts were the great
elements which carried convictions. He was never, to
my knowledge, a great talker. He spoke only when
he had something to say, and he never failed to have
listeners. Like his colleague, Judge Collamer, he had
great contempt for wordy pretenders; and he did not
think it the highest attainment of a statesman or a
scholar to be able to marshal words into high-sounding
sentences, with the superlatives in front. His example
to the aspiring young men of his State and country
was of inestimable value. He taught them lessons of
temperance, truthfulness, honor, and all the social and
moral virtues of noble manhood. He carried his
morality and honor into politics, and by his teachings
and example convinced the young men that honesty
and straightforward manliness is the best policy in every
relation in life. He did not believe in that miserable
heresy, that everything is fair in politics, and that the

scramble for office is a game that justifies unfair means
and falsehood. In this he and Judge Collamer were
much alike. The result of such examples and such
teachings is that Vermont has the purest political
atmosphere of any State in the Union. I consider this
no small compliment to my native State, and I claim it
as a great honor to her public men. Men in public
life are greatly responsible for the morals of the people.
Men in high positions exert a vast influence upon am-
bitious young men, and their examples are powerful for
good or evil. If they would all sternly and religiously
imitate the example of the two lamented senators of
Vermont, bribery, corruption, and political trickery and
baseness would be unknown, and we might all have
greater hopes of the republic. Two more pure, just,
and upright statesmen never graced and dignified the
Senate chamber. Both, in an eminent degree, combined the qualities that make the perfect man and
Christian statesman. The lives of both of them have
illustrated what we should all regard—that character
is the one thing valuable; that reputation, which is the
mere shadow of a man, is, in the long run, of infinitely
less importance.

Vermont has great cause for mourning. Twice has
she been stricken within a few months, and her two
most eminent and respected citizens have been taken
away, and are now buried in the shadow of her green
mountains. High position could not shield them, great
ability and moral worth could not save them, from the

arrows of death. They have gone the way of all the earth, but they have left bright and honorable records as a legacy for their own State and as examples for those who may occupy like positions. These noble men have conferred great honor upon their State, and the people thereof will long hold them in proud and grateful remembrance. The loss of Vermont is the nation's loss, and we do well to express a nation's sorrow. By this sad event, we who occupy these seats are called to contemplate the summons which will soon come to each one of us. Senators, behold the point towards which all human things converge—the grave. It is appointed unto all men once to die. A few brief years will bring each one of us to the end of life's journey and finish our earthly record. When we shall have arrived at the last moment of our existence here below, and the sight of the natural eye becomes dim, God grant that, looking heavenward, we may be able to exclaim, with our departed friend, "I see it! I see it! The gates are wide open! Beautiful! Beautiful!"

Address of Mr. EDMUNDS. *of Vermont.*

Mr. PRESIDENT: Were the aphorism of the great
dramatist true, that—

> "The evil that men do lives after them;
> The good is oft interred with their bones,"

there would be little, indeed, left to remind us of him
who has now so lately vanished from the council chamber of the nation and from this vast and majestic edifice
which has grown into stature and beauty under the
enchantment of his labors; he would stand with those
described in the sad but beautiful passage in the Divine
Comedy:

> "On earth they left no record in their day;
> Mercy and justice hold them in disdain;
> Speak not of them, but look and pass away,"

and his memory would pass with his mortal body
from the knowledge of men. But a higher philosophy
and a better religion teach us that, however it be with
evil, the good that men do is not buried with their
bones, but lives after them, ever growing, widening,
elevating, never lost, and casting its beneficent fruits
even into the lap of the remotest future. Whatever,
then, may be the sphere of usefulness and good to which
a man is called, or in which he moves, whether it be in
the loftiest regions of politics or ethics, or in the cold
and serene solitudes of abstract science, or in the practical administration of affairs, or in the humblest call-

ings of humble life, be his work well and faithfully
done, be his mission filled to completion, he has earned
an equal recompense, and has equally won the victor's
crown.

Thus, it has seemed to me that, on this sad and sorrowful occasion I may leave to other and more familiar
tongues the praise of Mr. Foot in his character of senator and legislator, and may fitly be excused from any
philosophical analysis, or estimate, or panegyric, of him
as compared with other eminent men; and leave to the
future the task of fixing, with impartial exactness, his
place in the high temple of fame, among the heroes and
worthies who have gone before him to their rest; and
the rather, as my heart prompts me, and as the wishes
of the people whom he has so long and so worthily
represented would, I am sure, direct, as his home friend
and fellow-citizen, dwell for a little space, as we mourn
at his departure, upon his personal relations to his people, and upon his long life of unblemished purity, and
of cordial and earnest love for, and pride in, his native
State, and upon his constant, and untiring, and successful efforts to promote their welfare and to realize their
wishes; upon his love of his country and of man.
Born to no ancestral honors, and reaching forward to
usefulness and influence only by the merit of his own
vigorous but unaided endeavor, he entered upon life
in perfect sympathy with the universal aspirations of
the people, and so, as step by step he advanced from
pupil to teacher, from teacher to leader, and from leader

to ruler, he was to them the type and example of re-
publican social progress—the representative man—and
all the people looked upon his successes as their own,
and felt in his advancement a triumph personal to
themselves. This affectionate sympathy of sentiment
was fully reciprocated by Mr. Foot. He took up, as if
by instinct, the feelings of the people, and never failed
to assert them against all antagonism. And these qualities of his mind and heart were not limited to geo-
graphical boundaries. He believed in the exhortation:

> "Love thy country and every other,
>   And wherever man dwells find a brother
>   Whom God hath related to thee."

So he was admired, and followed, and trusted by the
masses of the people. Whenever he was called upon
for assistance he individualized the case of each appli-
cant and made it his own; his heart warmed and his
face lighted up with joy at the opportunity of assisting
any, however humble, of his fellow-citizens; and hun-
dreds and thousands will carry through their lives the
pleasant remembrance of his grasp and smile as he
would dismiss them with encouragement and counsel.
Thus he endeared himself to men individually. His
sense of truth and justice was quick and vivid, although
his respect for sincere opposition was perfect, and so
he was not easily misled; thus he obtained the confidence and respect of those who could not gain his aid,
as well as of those who were the recipients of his favor.

His life was pure, generous, and blameless; free from all shadow of suspicion or reproach, and all who knew him had faith in his fidelity to his principles and to his State against all pressure and temptation.

And therefore on all sides there gathered around this earnest, fervent, hearty, patriotic man, the pride, the confidence, and the affections of his whole people, who now mourn his loss as an individual bereavement, as does he who now addresses you, whose relations with that noble man were of such affectionate intimacy and good-will as would make him fitly turn away and weep, rather than speak the language of deserved eulogy. In a busy, useful life he has filled his allotted sphere, and discharged his trust. "With enmity toward none, with charity toward all," he has lived and died. Mr. President, as we gather hope and wisdom even out of these sorrowful duties, let us remember that it is good deeds, and not the lingering years, that make up the full, true life of man, and that crown him with his best rewards.

Address of Mr. McDougall, of California.

Mr. PRESIDENT: I feel that I should not slumber well to-night without the utterance of one word to dignify the late senator from Vermont. Myrrh and frankincense were the symbols of praise in the old Hebraic, and that praise, it was supposed, went up above. There is another lesson in another school, perhaps as ancient

but not as anciently recorded, that the dead rested in
their caves until their praises were hymned by the
songs of bards, and then they were freed from their
caves and went to the heavens. It is my impression
that the late senator from Vermont was one of the
noble men who adorned this Senate, adorned our government, and distinguished his State as Vermont has
been distinguished. There is something in her pine-
clad hills and tall mountains that makes great men. I
do not know the man with whom I have met in the
tide of my own times who was better fitted for public
service than the late senator from Vermont. Every
one in the Senate chamber felt, when he came here to
present himself, whether in the President's chair or in
his own seat on the other side of the chamber, that he
was an ornament to the Senate, both intellectually and
morally. It would be difficult to convey in formal
words the due compliment that all of us owe him, to
give him the fullness of his merit. I feel it due to
myself, out of respect for him, his high office, and the
manner in which he conducted himself in his high
office, to say this much in his praise; and if I had a
harp like David I would sing to him as David sang to
Saul.

The resolution was unanimously adopted, and the Senate adjourned.

IN THE HOUSE OF REPRESENTATIVES.
THURSDAY, MARCH 29, 1866.

A message from the Senate, by Mr. FORNEY, its Secretary, communicated the following extract from its journal; which was read:

"IN SENATE OF THE UNITED STATES,
"*March* 29, 1866.

"*Resolved*, (unanimously,) That the members of the Senate, from a sincere desire of showing every mark of respect to the memory of Hon. SOLOMON FOOT, deceased, late a senator from the State of Vermont, will go into mourning for the residue of the present session, by the usual mode of wearing crape on the left arm.

"*Resolved*, (unanimously,) That the Senate will attend the funeral of the deceased from the Senate chamber at one o'clock to-day, and that the committee of arrangements, consisting of Messrs. DOOLITTLE, ANTHONY, HOWARD, HENDRICKS, SHERMAN, and BUCKALEW superintend the same.

"*Ordered*, That the Secretary communicate these proceedings to the House of Representatives."

Mr. MORRILL. Mr. Speaker, I learn that senators who desire to submit remarks in relation to the life and character of the eminent senator from Vermont, whose decease has just been communicated to this House, are not ready to do so to-day. The family of the deceased were desirous to reach home this week, and therefore the funeral ceremonies could not be deferred. I may also state that some of my colleagues are at the present moment absent; and I trust that at some early day the usual opportunity will be afforded for submitting such eulogies upon the character and public services of the deceased as members may desire to offer.

I present the following resolutions:

"Resolved, That this house has heard with deep sensibility the announcement of the death of Hon. SOLOMON FOOT, a senator in Congress from the State of Vermont.

"Resolved, That, as a testimonial of respect for the memory of the deceased, the members and officers of this house will wear the usual badge of mourning for thirty days.

"Resolved, That the proceedings of this house in relation to the death of Hon. SOLOMON FOOT be communicated to the family of the deceased by the Clerk.

"Resolved, That this house will as a body repair to the Senate chamber to attend the funeral of the deceased, at the hour of one o'clock p. m. this day, and upon its return to the hall that the Speaker declare the House adjourned."

The resolutions were unanimously adopted, and the House took a recess until one o'clock, when it reassembled, and the members, headed by the Speaker, the Clerk, and the Sergeant-at-arms, proceeded to the Senate chamber to attend the funeral services of Senator FOOT, after which they returned to the Hall and adjourned.

THURSDAY, APRIL 12, 1866.

A message was received from the Senate, by Mr. FORNEY, its Secretary, notifying the House that it had adopted the following resolution:

"Resolved, That the Secretary of the Senate be directed to inform the House of Representatives that the Senate, having listened to eulogies on the character and public services of Hon. SOLOMON FOOT, a senator from the State of Vermont, lately deceased, out of respect to his memory, have voted to adjourn."

Address of Mr. WOODBRIDGE, of Vermont.

Mr. SPEAKER: But a few weeks ago the distinguished senator whom we now mourn arose from his seat in the Senate and pronounced a most eloquent and impressive eulogy upon his colleague, who had been gathered to his fathers in the fullness of his years, crowned with private worth and public honor. And now before the cypress leaf is wilted, or the first gushing tear is dried, we are called, in the providence of God, to a fresher grief for him who so freely mingled his tears with ours at the death of Judge COLLAMER, whom none knew but to honor and love. At that time Mr. FOOT was apparently in perfect health. His constitution was unimpaired by any exposure or excess, and his splendid and almost unrivalled physical development gave promise of many years of vigorous and active life, for he possessed

> "A combination and a form, indeed,
>   Where every god did seem to set his seal,
>   To give the world assurance of a man."

In speaking of the life and character of Mr. FOOT, I shall simply attempt to do justice. Unqualified praise of the dead is never either in good taste or truthful. Human character is never perfect; at best it is only good in parts. Mr. FOOT was born in Cornwall, in the State of Vermont, in 1802. He graduated at Middlebury College with distinguished honor in 1826, and the same year became principal of the seminary at Castleton. He was tutor in the University of Vermont in 1827, and again, from 1828 to 1831, principal of Castleton Seminary, and by his earnest efforts and marked executive ability gave such an impulse and character to the institution that it ranked for many years among the first of the classical schools in Vermont. In the midst of his faithful and arduous labors as a teacher he devoted the time usually given to recreation and the refined pleasures of social life to the study of the law, and in 1831 was admitted to the bar in Rutland, and immediately commenced the practice of his profession. For five years he was a member of the legislature of Vermont, and for three years speaker of the house of representatives. From 1836 to 1842 he was prosecuting attorney for the county of Rutland. He was a member of the constitutional convention which established the senate as a co-ordinate branch of the legislature of Vermont, in which body he actively co-operated with his late colleague, Judge COLLAMER. From 1843 to 1847 he was a member of this body, and declined a third election. In 1850 he was elected senator of the United States, and occupied the position until the day of his death.

Such is a brief recital of the public and official positions occupied by Senator FOOT, embracing a period of nearly a third of a century. Born of highly respectable but comparatively poor parents, he was by force of circumstances thrown upon his own resources, and early in life acquired independent habits of thought

and action. Without any of the adventitious surround-
ings of wealth, of station or patronage, without any of
that extreme brilliancy of genius which now and then
startles and dazzles the world, he looked upon life as a
great reality, and upon success as the reward of labor.
He was rather solid than showy. He lacked genius,
but possessed talent and judgment. His qualities did
not shine forth like the greater lights in the heavens,
but there was in them a proportion and harmony which
gave a moral grandeur to the man.

    Senator Foot was what we call a self-made man. I
do not attribute to him any particular credit for that.
The term "self-made man" is a much-abused one.
There is no royal road to greatness. Every man who
comes to be a power reaches it through personal effort.
The scholar is self-made, and becomes a scholar through
patient and exhausting labor and reflection. The professional man is self-made, and so is the merchant and
the artisan. That Senator Foot succeeded where a
weak will would have failed is doubtless true, and
hence the greater honor to the man. As a lawyer Mr.
Foot was not learned. As a statesman he never seized
upon new theories or ventured upon untried paths. As
a political economist he never originated new ideas or
developed old ones with extraordinary power, and yet,
without question, he was one of the safest statesmen
and most judicious legislators of the age. He did not
resemble the mountain, towering to the skies, barren
and useless from its height, but rather the lesser emi-

nence. whose summit is covered with the forest, and
whose slopes wave with the yellow grain.   He did not
resemble the terrific shower, which destroys by its
violence, so much as the gentle rain, which the earth
drinks, and then dresses herself in new life and beauty.

God granted Mr. Foot one of the greatest of
earthly blessings, a loving, praying, pious mother, who
early instilled into his mind principles of reverence
toward God, obedience to authority, and love of truth;
and through a long public life the great leading char-
acteristic of his mind, and perhaps the highest power
of his character, was his devotion to truth—that high
ethical truth which is grounded in the moral being and
the fitness of things, lying back of and deeper than
refinements or popularities, reaching down to the inner
nature and elevating the moral forces. "His word was
as good as his bond." No social or political combina-
tion or influence; no sycophantic flatterer; no dastardly
and cunning insinuator; no expectation of reward, or
place or power, ever shook the truthfulness of SOLOMON,
FOOT.

Senator Foot was a patriotic man

"He loved his land because it was his own,
  And scorned to give aught other reason why."

He cherished the principles of the Declaration of
Independence. He believed that all men were created
free and equal, and yet subordinated his acts and theories to the Constitution of the land   Constitutional

liberty was his watchword; and when by force of law all men became absolutely free, he was the earnest and fearless advocate of those measures designed to protect the freedman in all his civil rights. But, sir, when the first gun was fired at Fort Sumter, and the cry "To arms!" echoed from peak to peak of the mountains of his native State, then the nobleness, the patriotism, the generosity of SOLOMON FOOT shone forth like a star. Calmly and serenely he met the issue, and everywhere infused into the people his own heroic and enthusiastic nature. And when at times during the progress of the rebellion the clouds seemed to lower about us, his faith in God and liberty never faltered. He trusted in the right. He met and performed every obligation of duty without fear and without reproach. The highest and proudest encomium which a public man can ever receive is justly his. Popular at home beyond description; elevated by the people to almost every office within their gift; beloved, honored, and trusted, he always and everywhere proved himself an honest man, the noblest work of God.

He loved his native State. To him there was no air so pure as that which swept about her mountains; no water so sweet as that which bubbled from her crystal springs; no grass so green as that which clothed her valleys; and he now lies beneath the shadow of her hills, where the wind sings his requiem, and the solemn old pines stand as sentinels over his dust. During the long and bloody rebellion, when suffering and death

entered almost every household, no wounded soldier,
no weeping sister, no heart-broken wife or mother, ever
called upon Senator Foot in vain. Their wants were
his wants. Their suffering was his suffering. In sun-
shine and in rain, in sickness and in health, by tender
and sympathizing counsel, and by active and efficient
effort, he labored for their relief; and we may truthfully
say for him, "When the eye saw me then it blessed
me. When the ear heard me it gave witness to me,
for I delivered the poor that cried, the fatherless, and
him that had none to help him. The blessing of him
that was ready to perish came upon me, and I caused
the widow's heart to sing with joy."

Mr. Speaker, it is a glorious thing to live in this
world. When its Creator launched it forth in the perfection of its beauty, the morning stars sang together
for joy. It was made for man, the last exercise of cre-
ative power—for man made in the image of God, into
whose nostrils He breathed the breath of life. It is
noble to live for the development of the soul. It is
beautiful to appreciate and enjoy all the works of God,
and all the endearing relations with which we are surrounded. It is glorious

> "To have
> Attentive and believing faculties;
> To go abroad rejoicing in the joy
> Of beautiful and well-created things;
> To love the voice of waters and the sheen
> Of silver fountains leaping to the sea;

> To thrill with the rich melody of birds
> Living their life of music ; to be glad
> In the gay sunshine, reverent in the storm ;
> To see a beauty in the stirring leaf ;
> To find calm thoughts beneath the whispering tree ;
> To see and hear and breathe the evidence
> Of God's deep wisdom in the natural world."

But more beautiful than life is the death of the Christian. Mr. Foot, from the commencement of his sickness, seemed to feel that he would die, and when the final summons came he was ready. His last thought was for his country, and his last desire to look out upon the beautiful sunlight and this noble edifice, where he had labored so long, and where he believed the future safety of the republic rested ; and then, as if fully satisfied, with eyes full of celestial radiance, he exclaimed, " I see it ! I see it ! The gates are wide open ! Beautiful ! Beautiful !" and the plastic form was stilled ; the casket was broken, and SOLOMON FOOT entered upon eternal rest.

Mr. Speaker, the life of a good man like that of him we mourn is not confined to its immediate and most apparent results. Its influence lives on, inspiring other men to lives of nobleness and duty. It is the pillar of fire by night and cloud by day, that safely guides us in our weary wanderings. Let us mark it well, so that when to us the last dread summons comes we each may.

"Go, not like the quarry slave at night,
  Scourged to his dungeon, but, sustained and soothed
  By an unfaltering trust, approach our graves
  Like one who wraps the drapery of his couch
  About him and lies down to pleasant dreams."

I submit the following resolution:

Resolved, That, as a further mark of respect for the deceased. the House do now adjourn.

Address of Mr. BANKS, of Massachusetts.

Mr. SPEAKER: The high respect entertained by the people of Massachusetts for the honored senator whose death has been announced by the Senate renders it proper that in this house, as in that of which he was a member, some tribute should be paid to his memory. It devolves upon me, in behalf of my colleagues and the people we in part represent, to discharge this duty. The State of Vermont acquired its territory from New York; but its early population was chiefly from New England. There has ever been between them and the people of Massachusetts an attachment that is due to common interests and origin. The anniversaries she cherishes are celebrated by us, in connexion with her sons, with the same spirit we give to those of the Pilgrim Fathers. In common with other States of the Union, we mourn this inscrutable dispensation of Providence that has deprived a patriot sister State of two sons so distinguished, so honored, so trusted, and so worthy, whose death she has been called to mourn. There is but one feeling, one manifestation: it is that of deepest public sorrow. Families suffer for the affection of mourning families, citizens the loss of statesmen and counsellors in whose experience and patriotism they were accustomed to confide, and the State sympathizes with her sister State, bereft thus suddenly of her most trusted servants and brightest ornaments.

It is but a short time since we were summoned to pay the last solemn honors to the memory of the senator of Vermont, senior by years, if not in service. We are now called upon to render a fraternal and public acknowledgment of the high honors due to the memory of the then remaining senator. There are few characters in American history more complete and perfect than that of Senator FOOT, or whose service has been more varied, satisfactory, or important. The public life of the late senator, it is true, was identified with the Senate of the United States, yet he had faithfully discharged the minor, but not less important, duties of local and neighborhood government which are so essential to the maintenance of our institutions and so closely identified with the destinies of the nation. He had been student, teacher, professor, town officer, representative, speaker, attorney of the people, constitutional legislator, and for a brief period, limited by his own choice, a member of this body. He had

studied the science of medicine and of law, the logic
and passion of popular assemblies, and, in the course of
his long and useful career, served his native State in
every public capacity, except that of executive or
judicial administrator of law. He had given much
time to public service in those public assemblies and
associations of the people which are unrecognized by
statute law, but which are of such paramount importance to good government. Knowing him as we do, we
can well appreciate how much he contributed, by his
benign influence, in these unostentatious labors, to the
prosperity and stability of the State he loved so well.
Such services are the foundations of the State. They
make forms of government practicable here which are
impossible elsewhere. They are the basis of American
liberty. It is in such duties that the people learn to
support, and legislators to direct, public administration.
We cannot overestimate their importance when performed by men of eminent capacity or station, and we
ought not to withhold from public servants the honor
due to those who faithfully discharge them.

It was not until Senator FOOT appeared in the Senate
that his reputation became national and his character
fitly appreciated by the millions that now mourn his
death. It is not distinction that they lament; it is the
loss of valued service. The reputation still exists;
with the lapse of years it brightens; but the capacity
for public service, now, alas! more than ever needed,
is gone forever. He entered the Senate in 1851.

That memorable year ushered in the most eventful period of our national career. Congressional history divides itself into three periods. The first is that of the immortal Washington. It closed with the administration of the second Adams. Every President, with this exception, and nearly every public man, had been numbered with the founders of States, the heroes of the war, or the fathers of the Constitution. It was the revolutionary era.

The election of General Jackson brought into operation new principles of action and new elements of power. The West, then limited, with the exception of Louisiana and Missouri, to the States east of the Mississippi, first asserted its power, and assumed to shape the policy of the country in contradistinction to that of the Atlantic States, north and south. Its mission was the development of the continent and the maintenance and perpetuity of the union of States. Secession and nullification were the enemies it first encountered. The intellect of Webster dissipated the metaphysical sophistries of secession, and the mailed arm of Jackson struck down at one terrible blow the hydra, nullification. Although presented under ordinary forms of legislation, it is now too apparent that the leading object of a portion of the people during the latter part of this period was the extension and perpetuation of slavery, or, failing in that, the destruction of the government. This struggle culminated in the measures of settlement in 1850.

It was in the succeeding year, at the very opening of the new age, that the senator we honor entered the Senate. The old parliamentary leaders were passing away. A few of the veterans still battled for a year or two, and then all were gone. New men had risen; old principles were to be affirmed with new zeal. The great States of New York and Ohio had broken the lines of ancient parties by unexpected and thorough revolutions in public sentiment, and sent to the Senate the present Secretary of State and the Chief Justice of the Supreme Court. Massachusetts suffered a still more surprising revolution of political sentiment, and was represented in the Senate by the senior member of her present delegation. Other States exhibited equally radical changes.

The South, though suffering no revolution in opinion, had gained in unity of purpose and intensity of spirit what it had lost in authority and talent by the change of leaders. It was too soon apparent that the bleeding wounds of the country, though assuaged, were not healed. Power had not won the prize for which it struggled, and concession had not secured the peace it coveted. Contests occurred in different parts of the country upon the execution of the measures of settlement. The compromise of 1820 was abrogated. Lurid flames of domestic violence and civil war appeared in the distant Territory of Kansas. The presidential contest of 1856 first disclosed the organization of sectional parties. States threatened secession. The flag of the country was fired upon by domestic enemies. Open rebellion ensued, and the most desolating and terrible war of all history was followed by the surrender of the enemy, the cessation of hostilities, the dissolution of armies, and apparent peace. Neither the place nor occasion offers fitting opportunity for the discussion of these great events.

The new senator from Vermont was called upon to grapple with the first and each rapidly-succeeding fact in the history of the unparalleled treason. Resistance to the purpose of the enemy, and the organization of measures and forces for the preservation of the country, opened to him a theatre that might have satisfied the highest ambition and the noblest patriotism. Never greater constancy, never higher wisdom, was demanded of man. In all this history the deceased senator, unshrinking, unselfish, and equal to the occasion, bore well his part. It is enough for us to say, turning down here the leaf of history upon his career, that none of his august associates, either of the earlier or later part of this great period, were more worthy of the high office he bore. It is not now, in this presence, undue praise to say that in the review of sixteen years of memorable senatorial service, amid complications and perils unprecedented in our annals, he has left nothing, in word or deed, that he can wish to blot from his dying record. He satisfied the country he served. He strengthened the cause he honored with his support. His labors were attended with constantly-increasing

success, and his life, rounded to its full period, closed
with the respect of adversaries, the confidence of constituents, the affection of friends, and the approval of
the world.

It would be unjust to claim for him in any especial
degree those brilliant qualities of mind or manner
which, in the judgment of some persons, constitute the
grace and charm of parliamentary life. It was his
apparent choice the approval rather than the applause
of listening senators to command. All nations have
regarded with pride the master-pieces of rhetoric and
passion, as well as of massive reason and diction, which
the world calls eloquence. Our countrymen, perhaps,
carry this reverence to excess. It is not by any means
the highest attainment of statesmen, and often is found
unaccompanied by any quality of mind or heart which
qualifies men for affairs of government. Speech-making
is scarcely a high art. It is rather what Dr. Johnson
calls it—a knack. It is not comparable in real importance with the power of conversation or of debate in
its true sense, still less capacity for administration.
Exuberance, and even extravagance, of speech, however, are the counterpart and accompaniment of liberty.
A vice in individuals it may be, but it is the image of
virtue in an age. But it is not in itself power, nor the
accompaniment of power. Power exists in integrity
and truth. Rhetoric sustains as well the apparent as
the real cause. Great rulers have been almost invariably silent, thoughtful men. If it were well to gild

refined gold or paint the lily, we might add to the
majesty of great actions the affluence and ornament of
exuberant and eloquent diction. But the senator we
mourn never failed in strong logic, convincing illustra-
tion, or intense reason, when it was required to satisfy
the world of the justice of his convictions or the wisdom of his principles. Speech in him rather served to
sustain than command the judgment. He had other
avenues to the human heart than those of imagination
or persuasion. He silenced adversaries and sustained
friends by more effective, though less brilliant, appeals.
He depended for success upon more enduring and nobler
qualities. Firmness of purpose, fullness of experience
and information, integrity of principle, constancy to
duty, purity of character, serenity of mind, correct
judgment, unflinching courage, and unceasing and honest
labor, were the weapons with which he won his con-
quests or turned or struck a blow. In him spoke an
earnest, intelligent mind, and the illustrious common-
wealth he represented. Individual capacity and representative integrity gave him authority and won for him
the unfading honors which will forever rest upon his
name. We recur with unalloyed pleasure upon this
sad occasion to the principles which adorned the life of
the departed statesman. Love of man and love of
country illustrated every act of his public career. It
is scarcely possible that it should have been otherwise
in private life. "For where was public virtue to be
found where private was not?" No trace of selfish

aspiration, of unmanly detraction, or sordid jealousy,
tarnished his official course. I do not know, in this
hurried estimate of character, what in him was wanting
that is necessary to the formation of a pure, patriotic,
Christian character. His life is proof that success in
public service is not inconsistent with strict integrity,
and that advancement does not always wait on dissim-
ulation and corruption. The manly simplicity which
distinguished him ought not, in this age of ostentatious
and effeminate luxury, to pass unnoticed. It was
neither complaisance nor austerity. His manner was
unchanged, whether in the Executive chamber, the
Senate, the committee-room, or the social circle. He
would have been the same to peer and peasant. The
ripe age to which he lived, his unimpaired energies, his
genial and generous temperament, his elastic step, and
the jocund health so constantly beaming in his open,
manly countenance, all attest the purity of his habits
of mind and body. They were those of the people he
represented. He could doubtless have shared with
pleasure in their mountain home—

> "A Roman meal,
> Such as the mistress of the world found
> Delicious, when her patriots of high note,
> Perhaps by moonlight, at their humble doors,
> And under an old oak's domestic shade,
> Enjoyed, spare feast! a radish and an egg!"

It would be the unanimous judgment of men that
such capacity and experience ought to be spared for the

direction of the generations that succeed each other.
But the law of Providence is otherwise; one existence
cannot span two lives. It is a consolation to know
that the senator we mourn lived the time allotted to
man, and that he died full of years and of honors. His
career is perhaps not yet ended. He who spoke the
universe into existence, who said "Let there be light,
and there was light," who created man in His own
image, and gave him dominion over the earth, may
have called him to another sphere for higher duties.
We may have yet the benefit of his love, if not of his
care. It is but a step from one life to another, which
all alike must follow, from the least unto the greatest,
until we are one with God! Happy it will be for us
if, in sharing the common lot, we close a career as long,
as useful, as honorable, as pure, as his whose loss we
mourn. The great struggle which opened and closed
with his career was finished. He had assisted in
removing from the escutcheon of his country the foul
stain that tarnished its lustre. He had fought the fight
and kept the faith. His name was honored among
men. He had received the highest honors of his State,
and of that Senate to which he belonged. He had
completed his work. Surrounded by family and friends,
he reviewed his life and settled his accounts with man.
He took his last farewell of those nearest and dearest
to him. He made peace with God. He was conscious
his end had come. He caught even from this side
glimpses of the blissful mansions above. He asked not

delay. What restrains the flight of that immortal
spirit? He has one thought, one last thought, more.
It is for his country. He is lifted from the couch of
death that his eyes may again rest upon its Capitol·
The massive columns, the extended wings, the sculp-
tured emblems of its progress and power, the rising
roof, the majestic dome, the Goddess of Liberty sur-
mounting all, and pointing the way he was to follow,
gave him the last taste of earthly pleasure! It is the
palace of the people, the symbol of Union, the temple
of Liberty, and with this sentiment impressed upon
his immortal spirit he passed from earth to God! May
his translation be to us instruction and example.

Address of Mr. WASHBURNE, of Illinois.

Mr. SPEAKER: On becoming a member of the House
of Representatives in the thirty-third Congress, in the
month of December, 1853, I first made the acquaintance
of SOLOMON FOOT, then a senator in the Congress of
the United States from the State of Vermont. I had
known something of his previous political history, and
was aware that he had enjoyed in a high degree the
respect and confidence of the people of his native State.
To possess the confidence and receive the support of
the citizens of Vermont is no meagre or indifferent
compliment. No State has ever guarded more carefully

the selection of its representatives in the national councils, for within my recollection no man in either branch
of Congress from that State has ever proved faithless to
liberty, or has ever had the stain of dishonor or venality
upon his garments. It is in the Green Mountain State
that there is to be found the type of the truest democ-
racy, resting upon the immutable basis of universal
intelligence and public virtue. In no State can be
found a loftier patriotism, a more ardent love of liberty,
and a more undying hatred of slavery than among the
constituents of the late distinguished senator from Vermont. When maddened treason raised its parricidal
hand to tear down the fabric of our government, and
the torch of civil war was lighted, the people of no
State rallied with greater alacrity and enthusiasm than
the people of the State of Vermont. Her brave and
hardy sons filled all her highways and byways; they
came forth from her hills and valleys, and from all the
gorges of her ever-green mountains, and marched with
the rapidity of the eagle to the defence of their imperilled country, and to vindicate the honor and the glory
and the unity of the republic. I say, sir, to have been
honored and trusted by such a people to the extent that
Mr. Foot was honored and trusted is one of the highest
compliments that could have been paid to a public man.
As has been stated, he entered the Senate in 1850, and,
being twice re-elected, served continuously till the time
of his death. Hence he served through the most exciting and turbulent period of our whole legislative his-

tory, and was a participant in the revolutionary scenes
which, to the philosophic observer, were the omens of
that terrible civil war that has drenched our country in
blood. I saw him in the Senate in the thirty-third
Congress, one of the little band of courageous and patriotic men who resisted with unsurpassed ability and
eloquence the repeal of the Missouri compromise. I
saw him when the slaveholders, in the pride and inso-
lence of their power, undertook to "crush out" in the
Senate every aspiration for liberty, and every noble and
elevated sentiment of freedom; when treason, upheld
by a perfidious and treacherous Executive, stalked
through the Senate hall with brazen impudence, and
when the galleries howled their applause of traitors.
Undaunted and undismayed, while all the political elements were lashed into fury around him, he bore himself in a manner becoming an American senator, and
courageously vindicated his own opinions and the sentiments and convictions of his own liberty-loving constituents. From his long association and thorough
acquaintance with the southern senators, Mr. Foot
early fathomed their wicked designs and their treason-
able purposes, and from the moment those purposes
found an utterance in the hostile cannon that opened
upon Fort Sumter, his heart and soul, his thoughts and
his energies, were all given to his country. With a loy-
alty so devoted and uncompromising, with a love of
country amounting to a passion, he everywhere de-
nounced treason and its aiders and abettors with the

most vehement indignation. At the time of his death
he was the oldest member of the Senate in consecutive
service. Every year increased his reputation and confirmed his character as a steadfast friend to his country,
an enlightened statesman, and a wise and incorruptible
legislator. He was a man of education and intelligence,
of a vigorous intellect, and an enlightened understand-
ing: of giant strength and an imposing presence, he
was a genuine specimen of a Vermonter. As presiding
officer of the Senate for a long period he distinguished
himself by his promptness, dignity, urbanity, and fairness. He brought to the discharge of all his duties a
conscientious devotion to the best interests of the nation. Active, industrious, vigilant, no duty to his constituents and the country was ever left unperformed,
and so prompt and regular was he in attendance upon
the daily sessions of the Senate that it could be said of
him as the historian says of the younger Cato, " he was
always first at the Senate, and went out last."

Mr. Foot bore a prominent part in all our legislation
during the war for the Union, and his influence and
vote were always given to the most energetic measures,
and those best calculated to strengthen the hands of the
government in its gigantic task of saving the country.
To the administration of Mr. Lincoln he gave a warm
and. even an enthusiastic support. I had occasion to
know of the strength of his attachment to that distinguished man, and to know how gratefully his friendship
was reciprocated. Mr. Lincoln had not in the whole

length and breadth of the land a more earnest and sincere friend, and no man stood by him through all the perils and difficulties of his administration with more unflinching devotion, and the people of Illinois will cherish this remembrance with gratitude. And when the time came for the representatives of a great and heart-stricken people to pay the last tribute of respect and affection to the memory of their martyr President, it was fitting and proper that Mr. Foot, the *pater senatus*, should, as the chairman of the joint committee of the two houses, be charged with the management of the proceedings. Profoundly anxious that the ceremonies should be worthy the august occasion, he entered on his duties with zeal and enthusiasm. He devoted himself with untiring energy to the accomplishment of the purpose. No man understood better than he did what belonged to such an occasion, and he gave his personal attention to all the details, and saw for himself that nothing which was necessary to be done was left undone. The day was cold, stormy, cheerless. At an early hour Mr. Foot's duties commenced. The crowd was great, and the pressure for admittance was tremendous, and he had to exert himself to the utmost to see that order was preserved, and that the arrangements were properly carried out. And all who were present know how admirably and satisfactorily everything passed off.

Though it was my fortune to be associated with him in that duty, it is but just to say that all the credit of

the successful management of the ceremonies belonged
to him. After the proceedings were over, exhausted
and overcome with fatigue, Mr. Foot went to his lodgings, and that night was attacked with the disease
which terminated his life. I saw him at his rooms two
days after he was taken sick, and he then believed himself so far recovered that he would be enabled to go
with me the next morning to call on the distinguished
citizen who delivered the eulogy, and to convey to him
the resolution of Congress, requesting a copy of the
same for publication. He was not, however, able to
go, but sent his colleague in the Senate, Judge POLAND,
in his place. On the next day, Friday, the 16th day of
February, the late senator from Vermont appeared in
the Senate for the last time, and made his final report
as chairman of the joint committee of arrangements,
and his last motion was, that "the report and accom-
panying papers be printed." He continued to take a
deep interest in the publication of the eulogy and the
proceedings connected therewith, and the last official
act of his life was to approve a portrait of Mr. Lincoln,
which is to be the frontispiece to the volume of the
published proceedings.

Mr. Speaker, when we contemplate the great changes
that have taken place among the public men who were
associated with Mr. Foot when he first entered the
Senate, and since the time when you and I first entered
these halls, we are admonished how fleeting and evanescent are all things human. How few are left to

struggle on but yet a little longer, to buffet the waves and
encounter the storms and the tempests of political life!

"Apparent rari nantes, in gurgite vasto."

Vermont mourns the loss of her faithful and devoted
public servant, and the nation shares in her grief. He
followed, alas! too soon, him who had so lately been his
colleague. The mournful accents of eulogy pronounced
in this chamber upon the illustrious COLLAMER had
scarcely died away before we were called upon to follow
to the grave his companion, adviser, friend, so long associated with him in the service of the country. These
two great American senators, both alike eminent for
their Christian virtues, their eminent statesmanship,
their devoted patriotism, their long and useful public
services, and their unsullied integrity, have passed
away, and the places on earth that have known them
will know them no more forever. They have gone, but
they have left to the country the richest legacy in the
recollection of their well-spent and honored lives.

Address of Mr. JOHN L. DAWSON, *of Pennsylvania.*

I rise, Mr. Speaker, to second the resolution of the
gentleman from Vermont. In the discharge of public
duty the paths of the senator and the representative, of
necessity, lie measurably apart. Most of Mr. Foot's
political convictions were not mine. With such ob-

stacles in the way of intimate relations, either private
or official, I cannot, of course, reveal those finer and
higher qualities of his nature which great spirits like
his never parade before the world, and display only
upon impulse to the most sincere and affectionate of
friends. But I know of him what all men knew of
him, and I esteem it a privilege which any just man
might seek to add my voice to the universal exclama-
tions of sorrow which his death has wrung from every
part of the land. It is unnecessary to repeat here Mr.
Foot's long and arduous services in public place. The
country is familiar with his record. 'It is enough that
his own State kept him so long in the Senate that at
the close of his life he was regarded as the father of
the body—the oldest of all in continuous service. He
mingled in those debates of the Senate which the
common judgment of mankind assigns a place beside
the grandest specimens of classic oratory, when they
were conducted by statesmen who were the rivals of
Chatham, Burke, and Fox. He sat under the impetu-
ous eloquence of Clay, the terse and severe logic of
Calhoun, the rich and luminous periods of Webster.
He was there amid those portentous scenes which preceded the late civil war, when all hearts were oppressed
with the deep dread of coming disaster, when the
friends of free institutions in the Old World, and many
in the New, feared that the American Union was
crumbling into fragments. It was the mightiest conflict
that ever shook the earth. He saw from that high

theatre, as well of contention as of observation, the rise, career, and downfall of several political parties Of such long experience, full of years and full of honors, wise and prudent, pure and upright, brave but philosophic, surely Solomon Foot was the Nestor among his official peers. Few men's opinions were ever sought with more respect or received with more reverence than his. In the midst of a revolution, second only to the "reign of terror" which drenched France with blood, and filled her beautiful cities and gardens with the graves of her people, when all our fiercest passions were aroused, his counsels to the ends of moderation and justice, soothing and subduing the vengeful feelings of the time, fell like the voice of that "old man eloquent" under the gates of Troy. Though he was gifted with remarkable firmness of purpose, and his mind had a sort of Roman vigor, he was eminently a good and eminently a mild man. It may be said that he combined the modesty of a woman with the constant integrity of Cato. Of Mr. Foot's moral character I need only say that it was without and above reproach. He was fearless and determined in the assertion of a right; but he was equally careful of the rights of others. No lure and no force could seduce or drive him to the perpetration of that which he knew to be wrong. He had that judicial cast of mind which constrains its possessor to analyze thoroughly, with patience and perseverance, whatever is submitted for decision, and to eliminate, with unerring precision, all the elements of evil. If he had not been a great senator, he would have been a great judge. The circumstances of Mr. Foot's departure from this life were of too sacred and hallowed a nature to be detailed here. Conscious that dissolution was rapidly approaching, he showed the high qualities of his character in the religious fervor and the steadfast hope, which grew warmer and stronger as he died. To the very latest moment he shed upon all who entered his presence the inspiration of a large and enlightened soul. The last parting glance of the expiring senator was turned to the dome of this Capitol. He begged to be lifted that he might see it once more— the scene of his long labors, the spot where he had well earned the veneration of his countrymen—and then closed his eyes on the earth forever. It was the exhibition of the same patriotic fervor so eloquently expressed by Webster in his reply to Hayne. He rejoiced to see that the flag was still there, "full high advanced," the emblem of our nationality and the Union of the States. Mr. Foot has gone to his grave in the same soil with that other pure and honored senator of Vermont, who preceded him but a few months. It is said that amid the mighty mountains freedom loves to rear her brave and sturdy children. But no mountains on the globe, not even those of Scotland, which overlook the grave of Bruce, or those of Switzerland, which cast their shadows over that of William Tell, have ever kept sentry over the tombs of two nobler men or hardier patriots than do the Green mountains of Vermont.

Address of Mr. GRINNELL, *of Iowa.*

Mr. SPEAKER: The words of affection are few, and only those shall I utter. It is a pleasing reflection that my early years were spent near the mountain home of the lamented senator. He gave me assurance of his friendship; and that he cherished the memory of my dearest deceased kindred furnishes me an occasion to pay a brief and sorrowful tribute to his character and virtues. That biography which follows the eulogistic sketches in the forum will place the deceased in the front rank of our truly Americanized gentlemen and statesmen, the measure of whose success should be unseparated from the associations and means by which it was attained. The grave senator ever with emotion and pride spoke of the rural town of Cornwall, Vermont, where he was born. Its population is not a thousand souls, and less than at the beginning of this century, yet has the distinguished honor, in addition to an intelligent yeomanry, that of furnishing thirty-six educated clergymen, eighteen lawyers, twenty-three physicians, and fourteen professional teachers. Its town institutions were the church, the lyceum, and the school. In the church young Solomon was baptized; at the lyceum he spoke to give promise of future eminence; and the school he left to become a teacher and college graduate, later tutor, and founder and head of an institution of learning. He honored the vocation of the schoolmaster, and never wearied in giving this

humble profession credit for its devotion to a refined
civilization and the general welfare. With truly Ameri
can simplicity he taught our youth self reliance, and for
himself he owed nothing to wealth, the partiality of
friends, or the issue of campaigns. He regarded it as
fortunate that he was early in discipline to tread the
hard rough paths of life. He was proud of his origin,
and that filial affection of a fatherless boy for a doting
and devoted mother was an augury of future fidelity
and devotion to the national weal most fortunately
realized in more than a quarter of a century of service
and ending with one of the most glorious tributes on
record to the worth of parental instruction and the
reality and value of the Christian religion. As husband
and father he was doting and beloved; a scholar without pedantry; a gentleman free from the arts of the
courtier; brave in action without bravado; matchless
in volume and sweetness of voice; persuasive in eloquence, yet abstemious in speech; genial as a companion, unwavering in friendship; in society

　　　"Pure as snow where streams of freedom glide,"

A Senator and statesman,

　　　"I am as the issue to stem oppression's tide."

Wheeling needless of life's stream, he could not prevent the gaze of the multitude, and ever in the presence
of the claims of honor, mercy, and justice, his noble
heart was so moved that his life is a fitting accord and
representation.

> "His life was gentle, and the elements
> So mixed in him, that Nature might stand up
> And say to all the world, this was a man."

Bereaved and gallant people of Vermont, millions are in mourning with you to-day. Memorable in history and conspicuous by the service of your public servants, it has been your fortune to furnish a noble exemplar for the nation, reflecting in character the grandeur of your ever-green mountains and the clear waters distilled in the rugged cliffs by the purity and beneficence of his memorable life now ended. In the shadow of the shaft of the purest marble which will be reared to commemorate his virtues in the chosen place of his burial, he shall sleep with more than the honors of a martial hero, for here he met a mightier than earth's mailed soldier, the "king of terrors," and with a smile. With a premonition of an early dissolution, he was raised from his pillow to gaze once more upon this Capitol, and then, with mortal vision ended, to behold in its brightness the city of the living God, the home of the ransomed soul.

Mr. Speaker, the effort to enforce the lessons of such a life illumined by divine smiles would be almost a profane attempt. It has more than the award of the gods. *Sol crescentes decendens duplicat umbras,* and by so far as eternity is unmeasured by time will his setting sun add to the lengthened shadows. I would accept it as a high honor to have recognized the proffer of the service, which I would make, by the thousands in the west

who claim paternity with the sons of the mountains who
have left the old house-tree, in being their honored servant in bearing the flowers of affection from the prai-
ries, the valley, and the mountains, moistened with their
tears in memory of a friend who now sleeps in sepul-
ture among the people whom he faithfully served, and
by whom he was so ardently loved.

Address of Mr. MORRILL, of Vermont.

Mr. SPEAKER: Never before in the history of our
government has a State been called upon to mourn the
loss of both its senators at a single session of Congress.
Vermont weeps, for her senators are not.   Only a few
days since and our tributes of sorrow bedewed the
grave and wreathed the memory of Collamer, whose
unblemished career had conferred honor not only upon
his State, but upon our whole country.   Then the
senator whose decease we now mourn spoke, in un-
broken health and strength, of the life and many virtues
of his late illustrious associate in terms of great fulness
and rare beauty; but how remote from him was the
suspicion that in so brief a time his survivors would
be called upon to delineate his own character, his
private worth, and public services, not less conspicuous,
and, though much unlike, moving in orbits widely
apart, equally meritorious.   Seldom has any State been

represented by the same senators for so long a time, and still more seldom so fittingly represented by those of so much eminence and unquestioned integrity and ability.

My colleague (Mr. Woodbridge) has so happily and eloquently portrayed the history of Senator Foot, while others have so generously acknowledged his worth, that little more remains for me to contribute. Like many men who have risen to distinction in after life, (to copy his own language applied to another,) "he owed nothing at all to the factitious aids or the accidental circumstances of birth, or fortune, or family patronage." Having lost his father at the early age of seven years, he was indebted to an excellent and pious mother for his early training and instruction, and for the foundation of those high-toned principles of honor and integrity which always guided him as a private citizen and distinguished him as a public man. Not born to affluence, he was while yet a boy taught the lesson of earning his bread by the sweat of his brow. An incident at this time shows that his ambition had early been touched by the ethereal fire. A man with whom he lived for a short time, when about fourteen years of age, sent him with a team to "drag" in some seed sown the previous day. Along in the middle of the forenoon the team was discovered without a driver, and the work accomplished appeared very inconsiderable. At last young Foot was found in a corner of the fence, lying flat on the grass. To the question as to what he was doing there he replied, "I am thinking what I shall say when I get to be a member of Congress." Thus "the child is the father of the man." If any of these field thoughts ever found utterance in Congress, they had not to wait much longer than those said to have been conceived in the early morning on the ramparts of Quebec, and which, many years after, embellished one of the most memorable speeches of Daniel Webster.

While yet a young man, Mr. FOOT often represented Rutland, the place of his residence, in the legislature of Vermont, and nearly as often was made speaker of the house of representatives; and here he first displayed his extraordinary aptitude for the discharge of the duties of a presiding officer over a deliberative assembly. This faculty was soon discovered and early recognized in the Senate of the United States, where he was repeatedly elected to the office of President *pro tempore*, and where he was, perhaps, more frequently called to the duties of the chair than any other senator. It is just to say that much of the dignity ascribed, as well as properly pertaining, to that branch of Congress may be credited, for the last fifteen years, to Senator FOOT's high example of decorum, order, and thorough knowledge of parliamentary routine. He despatched business with admirable promptness, with equal fairness and grace, and he held at all times both Senate and the galleries under complete control by his commanding presence and his most un-

mistakable emphasis. His call to order, like the sound
of a trumpet, was heard and heeded. From his
decisions of parliamentary law there was no appeal
asked or desired. His dignified bearing and urbanity
during his service in the chair, as well as in the faithful
discharge of all other senatorial duties, his massive
features and courtly manners, will cause him to be
associated with and long remembered as a prominent
figure—a representative man—of the Senate of the
United States. He will also be remembered as one of
the last of those who entered the field of statesmen
while the great men of the last generation—Webster,
Clay, and Calhoun—yet lingered on the stage.

His speeches while in this house on the Mexican war,
in 1846 and 1847, were able and fearless expositions of
its origin and character, and received the hearty approval of a large proportion of the northern people.
In the Senate not all of his speeches have been reported in the Globe; certainly one of his best never
appeared, for the reason that he retained the report for
revision until it was too late to be inserted. His
patriotism enfolded his whole country, and, bidding
defiance to all party ties, when the honor and glory of
his country seemed imperilled, he roused all the energies
of his impassioned nature, and rushed to the rescue.
This temper appeared in his speech, in 1856, on the
Central American question, when England exhibited
her traditionary ambition for universal empire, by her
pretensions connected with Honduras. He said:

"Standing in opposition as I do to the present national administration; differing from it as I do most widely and radically upon
almost every question of domestic policy, I am the more happy in
being able to accord to it the tribute, worthless though it may be, of
my sincere and entire approval of the position it has taken upon this
question. However we may be divided among ourselves, however
we may contend and wrangle upon questions of domestic interest
and of local policy, yet, when it comes to a question with a foreign
power, wherein our national honor and our national interest are con-
cerned, as in the present instance, let us exhibit to the world the
beautiful and sublime spectacle of a great, a united, a harmonious
people; a people having one mind, one heart, and one purpose."

Among the speeches reported, that upon the Kansas
constitution, better known as the "Lecompton swin-
dle," was one of his best, and of marked excellence.
The plot to force a pro-slavery constitution upon a free
people was shown up with all its revolting features.
Not a frequent speaker in the Senate, he was yet
always listened to with attention when he did speak
upon any subject; and upon those subjects immediately
confided to his charge he possessed its entire confidence. His recent eulogy upon his deceased colleague
was not only worthy of the occasion, but was a good
specimen of the senator's matter and manner, and when
delivered awakened responsive chords in the hearts of
all hearers by its impressive eloquence and chastened
beauty. As a public speaker before a public audience
Mr. FOOT occupied no mean rank. His noble figure
and full-toned voice at once arrested attention. Never
begrudging preliminary preparation, his speeches were

clear, forcible, and well sustained to the end. His style never lacked elevation, and, without being ornate, was affluent and scholarly. Though admirable in temper, he could yet employ invective at times with crushing effect, and declaimed with the daring impetuosity of a master who felt able to both ride and guide the storm he was creating. But his great strength lay in his absolute earnestness. His voice gave forth no uncertain sound. No man ever heard him speak and went away in doubt as to his meaning, or as to which side of the argument he had espoused. Having satisfied his own judgment that he was right, he embarked his whole soul and strained every nerve in the effort to bring his audience to the same conclusions with himself. He was both sincere and positive, and utterly incapable of guile or double-dealing. His integrity, moral and political, was as firmly fixed as the mountains beneath whose shadow he was born, and there was never any doubt or speculation upon any question as to where he would be found. When he spoke, therefore, he brought to bear not only cogent argument, but the influence of a true man, the weight of an experienced legislator.

As chairman of the Committee on Public Buildings he had for a long period taken a deep interest in the work of the Capitol extension. His ideas were liberal—coextensive with the grandeur of the nation— and he would build well and for all time. He felt a pride in the splendors of the structure, fondly contemplated the time of its completion in all its parts, when all the vacant niches as well as the old hall of the House of Representatives should be filled with the statues of our fathers, when the surrounding grounds should be enlarged, and believed in the end the world would not be able to show government buildings and grounds more imposing or so appropriately magnificent. It was the Capitol of a nation of freemen! What wonder, then, that he should in his last hour close the drama by wishing to be so raised in his bed that his eyes might once more behold the rays of the morning sun glittering upon the majestic dome and illumining those halls wherein he had long been so noted an actor. He was a modest man, and obeyed the gospel precept, "not to think of himself more highly than he ought to think," and esteemed "others" better than himself. Few men who spoke so well have been able to content themselves with speaking so unfrequently. He always appeared to underrate his own performances, and never, I believe, circulated any of his speeches in pamphlet form, but he was generous and hearty in his appreciation and circulation of those made by others.

He was a man of courage. When he served in this house, belonging to the old Whig party, the great radical abolitionist from the Ohio Ashtabula district was also a member. Anti-slavery sentiments in those days found little favor anywhere, and here encountered fiercest hate and frequent violence on the part of slaveholding representatives. Mr. Giddings

once told me that upon one occasion, when he had
uttered some unwelcome truth about the institution of
barbarous memory, one of these chivalric representatives rushed toward him evidently bent on mischief, and
that Foot at once sprang to his side ready to meet the
aggressor. The promptness of this action and the firm
port of Mr Foot awed the would-be assassin, and he
retired to his seat. Nobody, said Mr. Giddings, could
doubt the meaning of the one or the other.

The delicate as well as difficult duty of making up
the various committees of the Senate frequently fell to
his lot, and it was always performed with great discretion and fairness. Here his modesty was apparent, for
he never so carved as to leave the choicest parts to
himself. Mr. Foot was industrious, methodical, punctual to all appointments, and never postponed the work
of to-day for the greater leisure of to-morrow. Whatever he aimed to do he aimed to do well.

He was proud of Vermont, loved her history, and
wore her honors worthily. But he was not too proud
to labor for the humblest of his constituents, and by
his labors he added lustre to his State and honor to the
nation.

If it be that God loves those who are ready for his
coming "in such an hour as ye think not," or those He
takes while yet in the full enjoyment of their strength
and hopes, with mind and reputation as well as faith in
the grace of God undimmed, then was Senator Foot
fortunate as he was happy in the time of his death.

Life was at its acme, and he filled as large a space in the world as his highest ambition had ever coveted. He had not tired himself, nor was the world tired by his presence, but he seemed to see, as with a heavenly vision, a welcome awaiting him in the new world to which he was hastening, and exclaimed, "I see it! I see it! The gates are wide open! Beautiful! beautiful!"

Senator Foot was pre-eminently a large-hearted man, nursing no ill-natured jealousies in himself nor in others; far less did he indulge in any malice, and was the readiest man I have ever known to forget and forgive a seeming neglect or actual injury. Opponents never found his tongue lubricated by the serpent's poison, nor did friends ever find themselves "damned by faint praise," for he was lukewarm in nothing, but distributed praise and blame openly, manfully, and with a most refreshing unction. For his friends he was ready to make any sacrifices, and he obeyed their behests with a cordial alacrity never to be forgotten by those whom his position, official or other, enabled him to assist. Our volunteer soldiers and officers, so suddenly called from industrial avocations to put down the great rebellion, received his homage and tenderest solicitude. Of these he felt that the dead were all martyrs, the living all heroes, and his gratitude was unbounded. In his own State no public man ever possessed more of the affection of the people, as was sufficiently shown by his almost unanimous election by the Vermont legislature for a third term to the Senate of the United States.

He always met his colleagues with the most cordial salutations; no ill-wind ever rippled over the surface of their intercourse, and the most genial and affectionate relations were maintained up to the latest moments of his life. His loss to his family is irreparable, and so profound is their grief as to find no solace save in the contemplation of the dying senator's Christian faith. The last utterances of great men are often treasured up and serve to prove the strength of some ruling, possibly petty, passion of the deceased; but rarely have the last words of any man been so fit to be reported to the world, or such as to be more likely to be forever engraven on the hearts of his friends, than those of the lamented Senator Foot. Without an enemy in the world, loving God, and glowing with affection for all, and especially for those who visited him in his last hours, with eyes still beaming with all their wonted brilliancy, his unimpassioned words, so clearly articulated, so lovingly tendered, were well calculated to touch every heart by their wonderful pathos.

Honored senator! true patriot! faithful friend! farewell!

The resolution was adopted, and the House adjourned.

.

www.ingramcontent.com/pod-product-compliance
Lightning Source LLC
Chambersburg PA
CBHW030626270326
41927CB00007B/1324

*9 7 8 3 3 3 7 1 7 5 0 5 4 *